Huici

Elizabeth L...

...e STRECKMYRE

...çoise Jamicot

Gudrun Malka

E. Aube

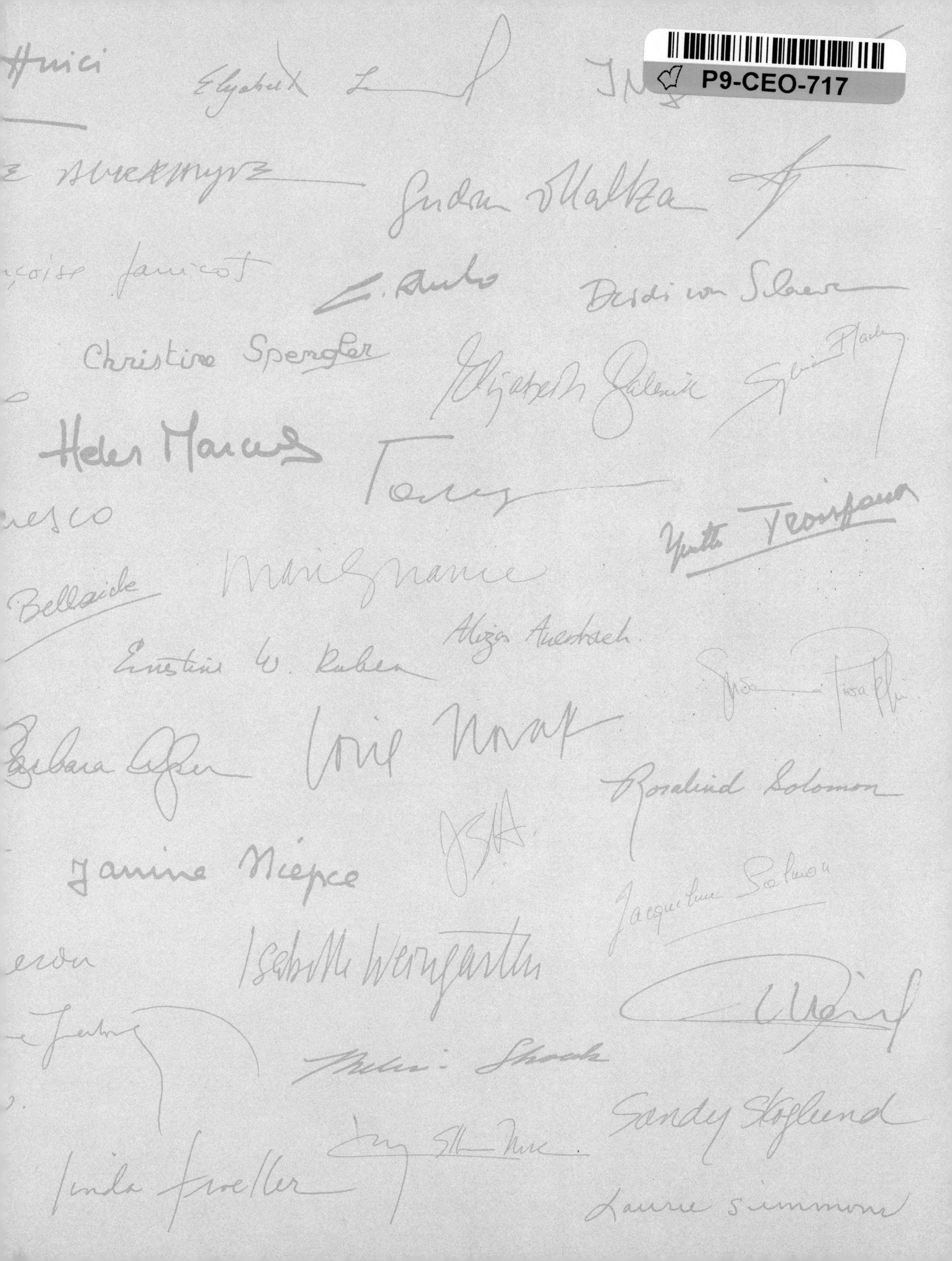

Christine Spengler

Desdi von Schaewen

Elizabeth ...

Sylvia Plach...

Helen Marcus

Torres

Yvette Troispoux

...resco

Bellaide

Mariegnarie

Alison Auerbach

Ernestine W. Ruben

Susan Pisa...

Barbara Afken

Lorie Novak

Rosalind Solomon

Janine Niepce

JSA

Jacqueline Salmon

Isabelle Weingarten

...erson

...Hartwig

Melvin Shook

Sandy Skoglund

Linda Froeller

Jay Satterwhite

Laurie Simmons

# OUR MOTHERS

PORTRAITS BY 72 WOMEN PHOTOGRAPHERS

EDITED BY VIVIANE ESDERS

# LIST OF CONTRIBUTING PHOTOGRAPHERS

**PAOLA AGOSTI,** ROME, ITALY ❖ *10*

**SUNG KEUM AHN,** SEOUL, KOREA ❖ *12*

**CLAUDE ALEXANDRE,** PARIS, FRANCE ❖ *14*

**BARBARA ALPER,** NEW YORK, NEW YORK ❖ *16*

**EMILY ANDERSEN,** LONDON, ENGLAND ❖ *18*

**RAYMONDE APRIL,** MONTREAL, CANADA ❖ *20*

**JANE EVELYN ATWOOD,** PARIS, FRANCE ❖ *22*

**ALIZA AUERBACH,** JERUSALEM, ISRAEL ❖ *24*

**DOMINIQUE AUERBACHER,** PARIS, FRANCE ❖ *26*

**CAROLE BELLAICHE,** PARIS, FRANCE ❖ *28*

**ROSSELLA BELLUSCI,** PARIS, FRANCE ❖ *30*

**AGNÈS BONNOT,** PARIS, FRANCE ❖ *32*

**MARLO BROEKMANS,** AMSTERDAM, HOLLAND ❖ *34*

**CHILA BURMAN,** LONDON, ENGLAND ❖ *36*

**VITA BUJVID,** ST. PETERSBURG, RUSSIA ❖ *38*

**DENISE COLOMB,** PARIS, FRANCE ❖ *40*

**JUDY DATER,** PALO ALTO, CALIFORNIA ❖ *42*

**SIMONE DOUGLAS,** SYDNEY, AUSTRALIA ❖ *44*

**SANDRA ELETA,** PORTOBELLO, PANAMA ❖ *46*

**CORINNE FILIPPI,** PARIS, FRANCE ❖ *48*

**MARTINE FRANCK,** PARIS, FRANCE ❖ *50*

**GISÈLE FREUND,** PARIS, FRANCE ❖ *52*

**ANNE GARDE,** PARIS, FRANCE ❖ *54*

**FLOR GARDUÑO,** STABIO, SWITZERLAND ❖ *56*

**NAN GOLDIN,** NEW YORK, NEW YORK ❖ *58*

**EKATERINA GOLITSYNA,** MOSCOW, RUSSIA ❖ *60*

**DEBORAH HAMMOND,** SAN FRANCISCO, CALIFORNIA ❖ *62*

**TANA HOBAN,** PARIS, FRANCE ❖ *64*

**SARA HOLT,** PARIS, FRANCE ❖ *66*

**IRINA IONESCO,** PARIS, FRANCE ❖ *68*

**FRANÇOISE JANICOT,** PARIS, FRANCE ❖ *70*

**MARION KALTER,** PARIS, FRANCE ❖ *72*

**BARBARA KASTEN,** NEW YORK, NEW YORK ❖ *74*

**JASCHI KLEIN,** HAMBURG, GERMANY ❖ *76*

**JO LEGGETT,** SAN FRANCISCO, CALIFORNIA ❖ *78*

**ANNIE LEIBOVITZ,** NEW YORK, NEW YORK ❖ *80*

**ELIZABETH LENNARD,** PARIS, FRANCE ❖ *82*

# OUR MOTHERS

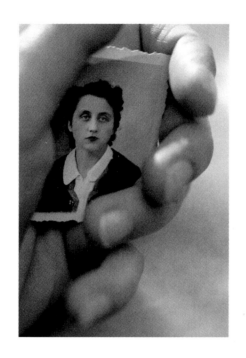

Library of Congress Cataloging-in-Publication Data
Our mothers : portraits by 72 women photographers / edited by Viviane Esders
       p.   cm.
     ISBN 1-55670-442-9 (hc : alk. paper)
      1. Mothers—Portraits.   2. Mothers and daughters.
    3. Women photographers.   I. Esders, Viviane.
TR681.M67093   1996
779' .24' 082—dc20                    95-40779
                                          CIP

Published in 1996 by
STEWART, TABORI & CHANG,
a division of U.S. Media Holdings, Inc.
575 Broadway, New York, NY 10012

Distributed in Canada by General Publishing Co., Ltd.
30 Lesmill Road, Don Mills, Ontario, Canada M3B 2T6

Distributed in the U.K. by Hi Marketing
38 Carver Road, London SE24 9LT, England

Distributed in Australia and New Zealand by Peribo Pty Ltd.
30 Beaumont Road, Mount Kuring-gai, NSW 2080, Australia

Edited by Linda Sunshine and Mary Kalamaras
Designed by Mary Tiegreen and Melanie Random

Printed in Singapore
10  9  8  7  6  5  4  3  2  1

**ARIANE LOPEZ-HUICI,** NEW YORK, NEW YORK ❖ *84*

**LEA LUBLIN,** PARIS, FRANCE ❖ *86*

**MARI MAHR,** LONDON, ENGLAND ❖ *88*

**DOLORÈS MARAT,** PARIS, FRANCE ❖ *90*

**HELEN MARCUS,** NEW YORK, NEW YORK ❖ *92*

**CORINNE MARIAUD,** PARIS, FRANCE ❖ *94*

**MARY ELLEN MARK,** NEW YORK, NEW YORK ❖ *96*

**SHEILA METZNER,** NEW YORK, NEW YORK ❖ *98*

**INGE MORATH,** ROXBURY, CONNECTICUT ❖ *100*

**MARILYN NANCE,** BROOKLYN, NEW YORK ❖ *102*

**JANINE NIÈPCE,** PARIS, FRANCE ❖ *104*

**LORIE NOVAK,** BROOKLYN, NEW YORK ❖ *106*

**ELIZABETH OPALENIK,** OAKLAND, CALIFORNIA ❖ *108*

**SUSANNA PIERATZKI,** MUNICH, GERMANY ❖ *110*

**SYLVIA PLACHY,** WOODHAVEN, NEW YORK ❖ *112*

**CATHERINE ROTULO,** PARIS, FRANCE ❖ *114*

**ERNESTINE W. RUBEN,** PRINCETON, NEW JERSEY ❖ *116*

**JACQUELINE SALMON,** LOZANNE, FRANCE ❖ *118*

**MELISSA SHOOK,** CHELSEA, MASSACHUSETTS ❖ *120*

**LAURIE SIMMONS,** NEW YORK, NEW YORK ❖ *122*

**SANDY SKOGLUND,** NEW YORK, NEW YORK ❖ *124*

**ROSALIND SOLOMON,** NEW YORK, NEW YORK ❖ *126*

**LISSETTE SOLÓRZANO,** LA HABANA, CUBA ❖ *128*

**CHRISTINE SPENGLER,** PARIS, FRANCE ❖ *130*

**LAURENCE SUDRE,** PARIS, FRANCE ❖ *132*

**JOYCE TENNESON,** NEW YORK, NEW YORK ❖ *134*

**BERNADETTE TINTAUD,** PARIS, FRANCE ❖ *136*

**LINDA TROELLER,** NEW YORK, NEW YORK ❖ *138*

**YVETTE TROISPOUX,** PARIS, FRANCE ❖ *140*

**NATHALIE VAN DOXELL,** PARIS, FRANCE ❖ *142*

**GUDRUN VON MALTZAN,** L'HAY-LES-ROSES, FRANCE ❖ *144*

**DEIDI VON SCHAEWEN,** PARIS, FRANCE ❖ *146*

**ISABELLE WEINGARTEN,** PARIS, FRANCE ❖ *148*

**CUCHI WHITE,** PARIS, FRANCE ❖ *150*

**NANCY WILSON-PAJIC,** NOGENT-SUR-MARNE, FRANCE ❖ *152*

**BIOGRAPHIES** ❖ 154

**CREDITS** ❖ 160

# FOREWORD

Two years ago I started collecting old family snapshots. Not of my family, but photographs of strangers.

Weekend mornings I walk thirty blocks or so from my home in Soho to the flea market on 25th Street. I don't remember when the cartons of discarded family photos began showing up on the

dealers' tables. Sometimes there would be as many as five hundred snapshots in one box, representing the memories of thirty, forty, or fifty families. At first it felt a little intrusive to look at these photographs. Yet I continued, I guess with the hope of seeing something I recognized. As I scooped up handfuls of pictures and methodically went through them, I discovered that everyone photographs the same things: handsome young couples arm in arm, babies lying on blankets, old folks pausing while sight-seeing, smiling young men in uniforms. There were birthday celebrations, usually for the very young or very old, seldom the decades in between. There were summers at the lake, a camp, the Grand Canyon. There were literally hundreds of photos of people proudly posing with the family car. And always, the captured moments were happy ones.

Sometimes the boxes hold the fun of discovery and other times there is the sad-ness of lost memories. A photo is history. Trespassing through the lost-and-found boxes of snapshots at the flea market, I wonder what happened to those families. Someone cared enough and loved enough to make the pictures in the first place. Why were the photographs discarded? Was there no one left to treasure them?

Families are stopping places and everything else is transition.

This book is like an old carton at the flea market where family memories live. But only mothers are here. And we know who took the pictures and wrote the words. We see here daughters struggle to render their mothers truthfully. Most of us haven't tried to do this since we took up crayons in grade school and, with love and craving for approval, drew wildly out-of-proportion stick figures with large heads, lots of hair, tiny bodies and uneven arms under a loopy sun grinning in the sky.

All of the women in this book are professional photographers. Some had never before photographed their mothers. Clearly, many welcomed the opportunity to make an elegant portrait. Some chose to submit an old family photo showing their mother when she was young. Some had no choice but to submit an old photo, their mothers having died. Surprisingly, several women pictured their mother nude. One feels a reversal of roles as the daughter assumes the position of authority; she the photographer, her mother, the sitter.

Great portraiture is a search for character, caught in a look, a gesture, a tilt of the head. Character also lurks on the walls, in the drawers, on the shelves. Jacqueline Salmon finds her mother in the garden. Martine Franck presents her mother in her living room, eyebrow arched, needle poised. Marion Kalter chose simply to portray her mother's empty closet. Surprisingly few of the photos were taken at an extraordinary moment; powerful exceptions being Annie Leibovitz's picture of her parents on their fiftieth wedding anniversary and Sylvia Plachy's portrait of her mother after her husband's death.

In many of these photographs we see the daughter reflected because the search for character always returns to the photographer. How much more pronounced that becomes when the sitter and photographer are mother and daughter.

All of the pictures are about communication. Many of these are pictures of

ENERGY IS MY MOTHER'S MIDDLE NAME. SHE RAISED SIX CHILDREN, HAD A CAREER IN THE PHARMACEUTICAL INDUSTRY, AND IS A GREAT COOK, GARDENER AND SEAMSTRESS. IN THIS PHOTO TAKEN TEN YEARS AGO, SHE WAS MAKING DINNER FOR US. MY PARENTS WERE SELLING THEIR HOUSE. IT WAS THE LAST BIG MEAL WE HAD TOGETHER IN THE HOME WE HAD SHARED FOR TWENTY-SEVEN YEARS.

things left unsaid. We feel the passion and emotion of each daughter as she made or chose her photograph. Each voice reminds us that we do not find the time or courage to speak to our own mothers of the things that really matter. Perhaps because we do not attain the wisdom or the courage to do so until long after we have lived apart from our families. Therein lies the value of this book. It sends us back to our own mothers. There is much to recognize and be touched by in the family albums of other people.

One sees these personal pictures, made or selected by professional photographers, with the heart first and then the eye.

I am in this book and so are you.

Mom, I love you and thank you.

*Kathy Ryan*

Kathy Ryan
October 1995

# INTRODUCTION

Why did I decide to work on a book about mothers? Did it have something to do with my own mother, a friend recently asked. I replied "No. My mother doesn't  have a husband. My mother doesn't have a child." He was speechless. It may have been this answer that prompted my interest in asking other woman to speak about their mothers and to rediscover their faces through portraits. I asked one hundred women photographers from all over the world to participate in this effort and almost three-quarters of them were able to respond. Each was asked for a portrait of her mother and some text about their relationship.

This project takes its form within a precise and specific work frame: the confrontation of a daughter in front of her mother. To do this as a professional is difficult. Taking a formal portrait is not like taking a snapshot at a family gathering. Does one have the courage to face one's own mother, to sustain her gaze, to adjust the camera, and to examine her face at such close range? This emotional encounter can result in a "portrait of truth."

Photographing one's mother is quite different from taking a picture of anyone else. A few years ago, I remember being deeply moved by a photograph a friend of mine had taken of his father. In general, I did not like this friend's work, it was too studied for my taste, but this particular portrait was masterful and, to me, captured the essence of this man's father. That photograph launched the idea of my first book, *Looking for the Father*, a collection of portraits by men photographers of their fathers.

Every photograph, especially a portrait, represents an exploration. When face-to-face with one's mother, it is impossible to cheat. A daughter who photographs her mother is, in some way, also taking her own self-portrait. In the process, all kinds of emotions and feelings emerge: fear, doubt, misunderstanding, admiration, and love. Sometimes the intensity of these emotions culminates in a mental block. "I cannot photograph my mother," one photographer told me, echoing the sentiments of several others.

Why this refusal? Because confronting old age is acknowledging our own age. Mother, or the memory of the mother, as youthful, beautiful, or vibrant has changed; perhaps it involves facing one's own mortality. Today, through the lens, traces of aging, fatigue, or illness are revealed. Eye-to-eye, this image becomes a mirror, a reflection of one's own face and body in progress. A double fear is born of this act: getting old, and seeing the face of your mother as it has transformed with time. As one of the photographers pointed out, ". . . to portray someone so close to me could take many years."

Many other photographers said they had a portrait of their mother but none of these images was good enough to submit. Not good enough? For whom? I wondered. For the daughter herself? For the publication of a book? Or, perhaps, for mother?

Nevertheless, for others, this opportunity was a fascinating exercise which allowed them to reflect on the problem which touches all women: the mother-daughter relationship, the turning point in a woman's evolution. Roles change in the course of one's life: the daughter becomes a wife, a mother, and then a mother to her own mother.

Photography is a powerful tool of evocation. Perhaps that is why it is used in therapy. Once an image is taken, then developed, it has the ability to spark an internal dialogue and allow us to examine our own mental images. The photographs in this book accomplish this. The written testimonials give strength to the photographs. Thus, image and text blend together to shed light on the mother-daughter relationship.

Some women took photographs of their mothers for the first time, magnificent portraits of older women who are beaming with serenity, pride, openness, and inner peace. Other photographers used an old family photo to capture the essence of motherhood. Some of those whose mothers were deceased and who wanted to pay homage to them, have fabricated images to reveal their innermost feelings about mother, sometimes personal, sometimes symbolic—always fascinating.

These celebrations of our mothers from women of different generations, cultures, and races, offer a wide spectrum of feelings: respect, admiration, love, incomprehension, suffering . . . and even a longing for death. Carnal, spiritual, and profound, the bond which unites mothers and daughters is, by nature, indestructible.

*Viviane Esders*

Viviane Esders
Belleme, France
August 1995

# OUR ROLES
# HAVE CHANGED

PAOLA AGOSTI ❖ ROME, ITALY

Today my father is dead, my mother is eighty-one. I am haunted by the thought of her death, which may not be very far away.

In a school exercise I wrote when I was a child, I mentioned her hair, her nose, her eyes, her smile. If I had to describe her now, I would rather talk about her generosity, her naiveté, her tenderness, her love for art, for writing, for languages.

There was always the child in her. Our roles have changed, our friendship has grown and I like to think that by protecting her, I act a little like a mother for her.

My father left us in two days. When I arrived at his bedside, he was already unconscious. Holding his hand, I kept telling him: "Dad, I love you." Did he hear me? Did he understand?

His death still haunts me. Before it is too late, I want to say: "Mum, I love you. Thanks for being here."

*Paola Agosti*

# AN IMAGE
SUNG KEUM AHN ❖ SEOUL, KOREA

an image of origin
an image of human
an image of world
an image of suffering
an image of Buddha

# AN IMPOSSIBLE LOVE

CLAUDE ALEXANDRE ❖ PARIS, FRANCE

My mother did not want my father.
My mother did not want a husband.
My mother did not want any children.

But she got all of it and could not stomach it.
No desire, no joy, what could she have done?
She failed everything.

On her denials, I built—and destroyed—half of my life.
The other half was saved by my father.

Day after day,
a perpetual struggle against my mother's negative current.
I come so close to danger.
I come so close to death.
I try to take myself further
And I am not sure that I am able to.
In the end, what did we make of our love?
An impossible love.

# SWEATER GIRL

BARBARA ALPER ❖ NEW YORK, NEW YORK

W ould I pass the pencil test, I wondered as a "developing" teenager. Remember? If a pencil stayed in place under your breast, it meant you were a good size and needed a bra.

Was I going to be as big as my mother? She's a 34DD! In a subtle way, her breasts always seemed to be a topic of conversation. I didn't know anyone else whose mother was so big. And silicone implants didn't exist then! I didn't want to be as big as she was, but I couldn't wait to have enough to put into a real bra. I hated the stretchy training one, and being measured publicly in a department store was unbearable.

"I was a sweater girl!" she said to me proudly. "It made me popular. Men liked me."

My mother was also quite a looker, smart too. Her breasts weren't the only attraction, but they helped.

"If I were growing up today, I'd consider reduction surgery," she confessed. Even though she wore pads under the straps, the indents in her shoulders still remain, and her slightly curved back seems to have been affected by the imbalance of her body weight. Ah, the burdens of being a sweater girl.

"You look just like her," I was told. "You even have your grandmother's hands." But a sweater girl I'm not, though I did grow enough to pass the pencil test. And silicone doesn't appeal to me.

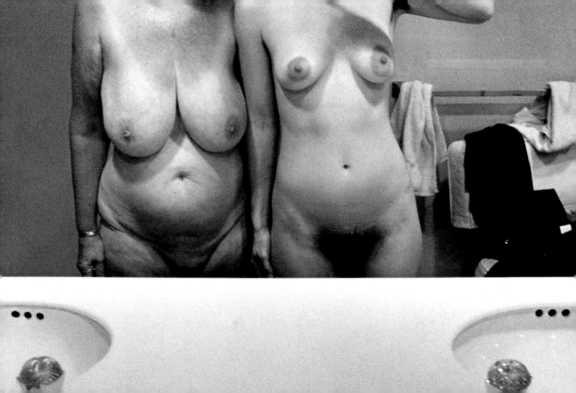

# ROLE MODEL

EMILY ANDERSEN ❖ LONDON, ENGLAND

My mother has always worked, from the time my brothers and I were born. She and my father have an antiques shop. I spent my childhood in salesrooms and junk shops, in open markets and at dealers' homes. In the world of antiques, there are many eccentric characters and many kind and special people.

My mother is an outsider. She was born in South Africa. After attending university, she, her mother and sister left to find a new life in England.

They lived in many small flats in London, moving often. At the beginning of the fifties, my mother taught young children in the poorer schools in the East End of London.

At the age of twenty-three, she went on a skiing trip with three friends to Méribel, France. They began their journey in Paris. Late that first night, after a whole day's drive, they stopped to have something to eat and then while driving down a long avenue they crashed into a tree. My mother went through the car window, breaking both her arms, her legs and her pelvis in eight places. She lost many pints of blood.

She was near death when a lorry driver stopped and drove her to Chambery hospital. A policeman there donated his blood to keep her alive.

A doctor at the hospital looked after my mother for eighteen months, piecing her broken body together during countless operations. He helped teach her how to walk again.

Through sheer will and determination, my mother survived the accident. It was like a miracle. She was told she wouldn't be able to have children and she'd be in a wheelchair by the time she was fifty years old. But she had my two brothers and me by Caesarean section.

At sixty-five, my mother walks with difficulty. I go swimming with her twice a week for exercise. She loves life and is optimistic and determined. She'll never stop working. Her family and business are the most important things in her life. I respect her resiliency and tenacity enormously. She has been an extraordinary role model, and we have a close and loving relationship.

Emily Andersen

# WHILE MY MOTHER SLEEPS
RAYMONDE APRIL ❖ MONTREAL, CANADA

In my memories of childhood, there is a terrible dream: My mother, my grandmother, my two sisters, and I are reunited in the house just like every night, but the house is void of furniture and detached from its foundations. It is floating in the abyss. Leaning on the window sill, my sisters and I are looking outside. But outside, there are no more houses, no park next to the church, no more church, no more neighbors, no one. Only the waves of black water and leaded glaciers, in the twilight of the end of the world. And it is the end of the world, without any doubt. My grandmother is busy with something. My mother remains close to us. She seems as petite as I am. She is also looking, calmly, in silence.

My mother has always remained a girl. Her love of life is as great as her anxiety. On happily routine days, she loves to squint her eyes at the sun, cut material for a new dress and put the potatoes on the fire. During the days of the big departure to Florida, she gets up at dawn and goes out into the fresh air in a woolen jersey.

It does her good to speak to the girls, in secretive tones, of insignificant and harmless things. It happens, certain nights, that she can't sleep because she is thinking of the children.

My parents are in retirement. They sold their former house when it got to be too big and settled into an apartment. When I'm visiting them, and it's night and I'm not sleeping, I get up and tiptoe into the kitchen. In the darkness, guided only by the numbers on the electrical appliances, I'm alone in a very strange exile. I feel my mother's absence so strongly even though I know she's sleeping in her bedroom; she's only resting in the room next door. I, however, am awake. I'm not used to being awake while she's sleeping. My throat's in a knot, like in my dreams.

*Raymonde April*

# BEFORE IT'S
# TOO LATE

Jane Evelyn Atwood ❖ Paris, France

My mother is headstrong. So am I!
That probably explains why we've
    often clashed.
One day, a friend whose parents had
    died, said to me:
"Try to get along with your mother.
She's the only mother you'll ever have."
I know that when she dies, it will be
    impossible to try anymore.
"Mama! Let's not wait until it's too late!"

My mother doesn't really like to be photographed.
This photo of her was one of my father's favorites.

# FOR ALL FLESH IS LIKE GRASS

ALIZA AUERBACH ❖ JERUSALEM, ISRAEL

When I was young and innocent, a very old and good friend told me something about the role of parents in life: "Parents are there to give and forgive." I thought this proverb would stand for ever, like one of the Ten Commandments. Little did I know then how right Heraclitus was when he said: "Panta rei"—*All things are in a state of flux.*

Time galloped forward and all of a sudden our roles changed. Now I am the one who must give and forgive. Not only as a mother to my own daughter, but as a mother to my own mother as well. It is not always easy to give and to forgive. But it is heartbreaking, even frightening, to realize how little connection there is between the sad, weak shadow I call Mother and the mother whose imprints are all over my personality.

My mother absolutely loved and adored children. She felt deep joy at seeing a tiny little flower bloom or feeling the warm sand at the edge of the wild blue sea where she used to swim every day of the year. She used to roller skate with all the neighborhood children. And her laughter. And her music. The Schubert and Brahms lieder she used to sing. The choirs she was part of . . .

I remember my mother toweling me after a bath, taking particular care with each little finger, separating them with a gentle touch in order to dry them without causing any harm. And now, here I am, giving my fragile old mother a bath, drying her as gently as I can, for she is so vulnerable, her body so breakable, her skin so transparent.

And her soul—where has it wandered? Only rarely do I still catch a glimpse of something in her clear, blue eyes. Mostly, I lurk in the dark, wondering where she is.

Yet there is still music. This is the bridge between the small, bent woman now sitting quietly in her armchair and the tall, beautiful mother she was once.

So I put on Brahms' German Requiem and place her thin hand between my own two. Isaiah's words quoted by St. Peter reverberates loudly—"For all flesh is like grass and all its glory like the flower of grass. The grass withers, and the flower falls." The music carries us to distant destinations, lifting our souls higher and higher until they reach those remote territories where words are superfluous and everything is brighter and clearer as we become one with the universe. Then, slowly the music fades and we descend into darkness once more. All that is left for me is to kiss her gently, to hug and caress her softly, and to hope that her spirit remains there, where there is no suffering.

*Aliza Auerbach.*

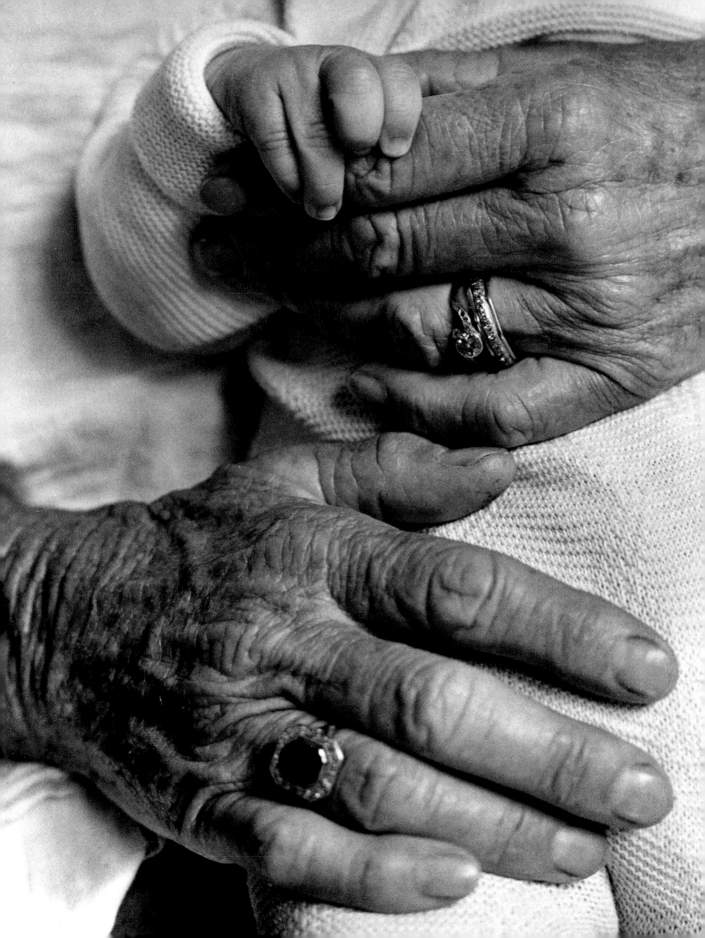

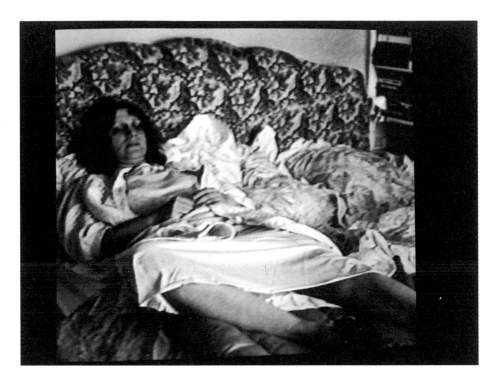

PHOTOS TAKEN FROM AUERBACHER'S 1993 VIDEO, *MA CROTTE EN CHOCOLAT*.

# FROM A MOTHER WHO LOVES YOU

DOMINIQUE AUERBACHER

PARIS, FRANCE

You're too headstrong. You do whatever suits you. If only it were possible to speak to you. You don't know what you want. Some day you'll be sorry, but it'll be too late then. Don't say I didn't warn you. I don't know who you take after, but it's not me. You have a hard voice and a wicked stare. Honor your father and your mother. It's not as if I expect anything from you, but have some respect for your father's memory. I have never been a burden to you. Not once have you ever said to yourself that I am alone. If only you knew how difficult it is to be alone. You are so unrealistic. You don't have a future. I'll have you to lean on when I get older. You can't just do what you want with your life. You really look awful. Do you have any money? Are you eating properly? Do you have enough money to buy food? You don't have a steady life. You don't look after yourself properly. I worry about you, but it's all over now. Your father was right. I do too much, I am too kind, for all the thanks I get! If only you knew how much I love you, how a mother's heart bleeds for her child. You are my flesh and my blood, flesh of my flesh. If only I could make you all over again, *ma crotte en chocolate!*

Listen to a bit of advice from a mother who loves you. You are always resisting. Your mind is closed. I know you better than anyone else. Just trust me this once. It's for your own good. You're not getting proper advice. Someone is turning you against me. I can see it only too clearly! You make it sound as if your mother were unworthy of you. It's too monstrous for words. You are really hurting me, you know.

Dominique Auerbacher

# RADIANT AND GOLDEN

CAROLE BELLAICHE ❖ PARIS, FRANCE

My mother has red hair and green eyes. It was the first problem I had to confront when I took her photograph: How could I make all these lovely colors come through? It is the first time I've used her as a model. And the first time I had to tackle the desire to reveal everything about my mother in one image; her liveliness, tenderness, strength, originality.

As she sometimes does, she behaved like a child. She was unaware of herself and having fun. When I looked at her, I saw clear eyes, full of innocence. As I took pictures, I discovered aspects of her I hadn't known—her clumsiness in front of the camera, the pleasure she took in playing with me.

We adore each other. It's only natural. I am the youngest of three daughters. She calls me "little one" but confesses she is still a little girl herself.

I am proud of her beauty. As a child, she slapped a passerby who bent down to contemplate her face. I am proud of her eccentricities, and amused by her fancies, from her collection of colored glass decanters to her love of the Russian language. One year, she studied Russian furiously, rolling her *R*s to the point of making us resent the entire Russian population.

She was born in Tunisia, and from the sun and the sea, she took her warmth and her liveliness. She is radiant and golden, like a small feline or an extraterrestrial being.

My sister says she is a saint. In all insolence, she is.

*Carole Bellaiche*

# IT IS NOT SHE
# WHO DISAPPEARS

Rossella Bellusci ❖ Paris, France

I hesitated a lot before agreeing to photograph my mother.

I was working on a project about disappearance, and it was painful to consider involving her in this concept. I would like to think she can transcend events, that she is not affected by anything, even my camera.

She helped me make up my mind. As we prepared for the shooting, I became less fearful. Behind my lens, I forgot for a moment that she's my mother. As a good Italian mother, she is not used to my directing things.

I wait for her verdict.

"You have made me look younger."

She accepts this image. I am happy and relieved.

It is not she who disappears. It is time.

# SHE LOOKS FORWARD

Agnès Bonnot ❖ Paris, France

My mother, a guinea pig for even the smallest experiment, is ready for anything, even posing for a photo. She hates it but is curious. She's ready to confide everything to me which she immediately regrets, without really regretting it. This is because she looks forward to everything.

She can make my migraine go away by placing ice on my forehead. She cures and appeases me. But sometimes I hate her—she loves my father or my brother or my sister more than me.

She changes without warning. She smoothes things over without taking sides. Moreover, she loves tennis. She is transformed on the court. She no longer hesitates for she has no one else to please.

Her presence is captured in her body. It is a tireless body, with the shoulders of an athlete, the hips of a Greek Ephebe and the backside of a black woman.

We all draw our strength from her. She, in turn, gets her strength from the earth which she moves, scratches, digs, rakes and hoes.

*Agnès Bonnot*

# RITES OF PASSAGE

MARLO BROEKMANS ❖ AMSTERDAM, HOLLAND

On the very day I was about to write this piece, I dreamt that my mother died.

I decided to perform the death rites from the Mayans.

It was like traveling back through time; an obscure atmosphere, dark forces, priestesses or sorcerers dressed in voluminous gowns, chanting strange formulas.

Afterwards, her body was placed in my bedroom, overnight. While I watched, her foot began to move. I thought I was hallucinating. But then her head moved, and the next moment, she sat upright.

I told my mother she had been dead, but I kept secret the rites of passage.

# ACCIDENTAL PHOTO

Vita Bujvid ❖ St. Petersburg, Russia

In 1961, Nikita Sergeevich Khrushchev took the liberty of making the following statement in connection with the space flight of Yuriy Gagarin. "The pinnacles of communism are already visible," said Nikita Sergeevich, and my mother, a naive and trusting woman, decided to provide herself with second child. So I came into the world.

My relationship with my mother is very complicated. And although it is hard for me to communicate with her, I always feel a strong bond between us. We now live in different cities but at a great distance I feel this bond considerably stronger.

I very rarely take pictures of people I am close to. I have almost no photographs of my daughter. I have never photographed my father. But I did photograph my mother once, almost by accident. I don't think she likes this photograph. As for myself, it is only because of this accidental photo that I have understood how my mother actually relates to me. If she sees this photo, I hope she won't be very upset.

The next time I see my parents, I must do something special, a photo made to order for my mother: in a favorite dress, or at the dacha, or with all the grandchildren—whatever she would like.

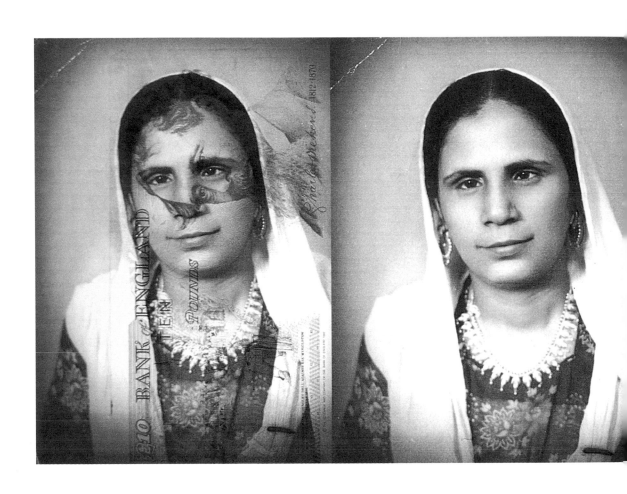

# EK PYAR EK DIL, EK DUNIYA

*THE SMILE YOU SEND OUT RETURNS TO YOU*

CHILA BURMAN ❖ LONDON, ENGLAND

My mother and grandmother, who is nick-named Tijou or 'speedy' in Punjabi, are extremely independent, powerful and positive women. I have spent many months staying with my nanny-ji in India. Like my mum, she is sharp, cute, fun, clever and confident. Both are singers, jokers, and serious entertainers at weddings and

parties. My mum works in Liverpool now.

My mum gave birth to seven children in harsh conditions of poverty, yet she still managed to bring us up with much love, strength and wisdom.

This work is a celebration of her survival. It is about reclaiming images of ourselves, moving away from the object of the defining gaze towards a position where we become the subject. The use of the ten-pound note superimposed over the image speaks loudly and richly about the nature of cycles and the meaning of money and people in the complex societies of colonialism and post colonialism.

It is an image rooted in one specific history.

*CK Burman*

# AN IMAGE
# INGRAINED FOREVER

Denise Colomb ❖ Paris, France

The following is an excerpt from the book, *Mon Siécle sur un Fil,* written by Edouard Loeb, my brother:

> "Our family was a happy one. My mother was in charge of watching over our studies. She was beautiful and severe, a woman of conscience as we call them, but her strictness was softened by her great sense of humor. Her straight nose, the precise outline of her chin, and her mouth, impassive, not a mouth for laughing: she emanated the nobility of the woman who does not give in."

I would like to add two personal memories: I must have been about fifteen. My mother was in bed, feeling slightly unwell. She smiled at me, and I thought I will always remember the image of her teeth, superb as pearls. It has stayed with me to this day.

Another image, on her deathbed: the translucent, smooth skin and an expression of softness that I had never seen before. She was ninety-seven years old.

*Denise Colomb*

# LIKE MOTHER, LIKE DAUGHTER

JUDY DATER ❖ PALO ALTO, CALIFORNIA

My mother is always right.

My mother knows what I am thinking.

My mother is clairvoyant.

My mother is proud of me.

My mother wants me to be happy.

My mother has a sense of humor.

My mother remembers dirty jokes.

My mother is strong and tough.

My mother is brave.

My mother is independent.

My mother is smart.

My mother works hard.

My mother is sentimental.

My mother loves me.

My mother is demanding, unrelenting.

My mother is jealous and catty.

My mother is unsentimental.

My mother has no idea what my work is about.

My mother wants to be waited on.

My mother is obsessive.

My mother is afraid.

My mother won't give me credit.

My mother gives me too much advice.

My mother worries too much.

My mother is never right.

My mother loves me.

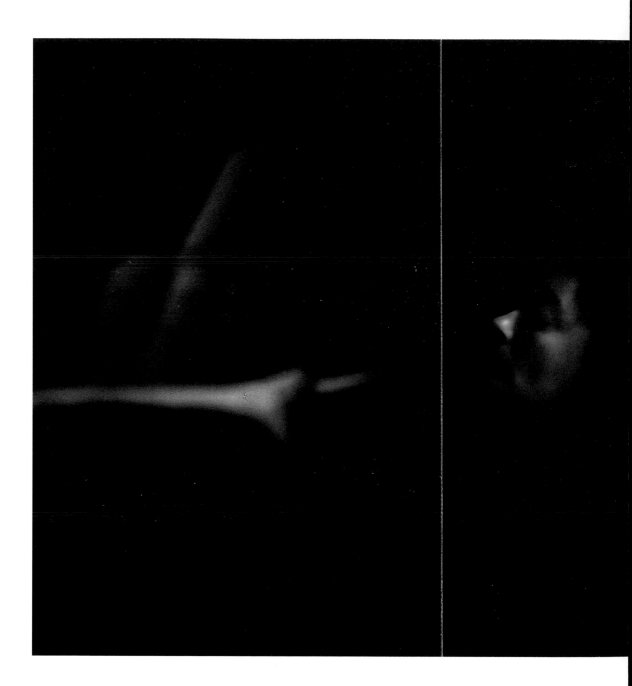

# LIKE A BREATH
# HARDLY DRAWN
Simone Douglas ❖ Sydney, Australia

The relationship between my mother and I
is tenuous
Like a breath hardly drawn
but precious none the less

# HOMECOMING

SANDRA ELETA ❖ PORTOBELO, PANAMA

Taking a picture of my mother is much more than clicking the shutter. Finding her eyes through the viewfinder is like arriving at a long awaited appointment. It is the homecoming after the journey away from her.

In the longing to find our true selves and our true intentions, we sometimes have to destroy the chains of tradition that no longer fit our nature. So we open the cage and sing our song in unchartered territory, carrying with us the memories of a faceless mother and a home which no longer shelters us.

The mother who tries desperately to win us back on her terms now sees only the shadow of a faceless child running, a renegade embarked on a journey she can't understand. So we become the shadow of the other, strangers trying to find in the other what can only be found within. After enough rain and sun have fallen on our faces, something starts to germinate, a trembling seed opens up after we move through the pain to the other side. It flowers in that space within, where the freedom of spirit clears our vision and makes us see there is no winning or losing. There is just enough love to forgive and enough love to accept ourselves and therefore make friends with the best friend we could ever find.

*Sandra Eleta*

My mother with Evelyne and Corinne.
Shot by my father, Le Mont-Dore, 1947.
Print by Corinne Filippi, Paris, 1993.

# AT THE END OF THE HALLWAY

CORINNE FILIPPI ❖ PARIS, FRANCE

In thinking about my mother, a whole palette of memories, sensations and emotions comes to me.

She was in and out. Quickly, in and out. Her days were made up of hard labor. I would wait for her behind the door, at the end of the hallway. As a child, my ties to her were woven out of this wait; out of a gaping, unsatisfied need. There behind the door, at the end of the hallway, I waited for her and created images. Stills from a film stopped short, right here, before it even began. Dark images that bore within them a promise of my coming to light, something I wouldn't realize until much later. Inside, as a little girl, I knew about the obscure and the bright, the dark and the light, about waiting and living.

Her speed, her energy, her need always to be doing something took me aback.

I remember, too, how she loved to laugh when she could steal the time, or when her laughter helped overcome routine. She loved to guess where the people walking by the house had been born. That way she could spot others who, like herself, were transplanted. She was the one who taught me not to reject people of different colors, to be curious and open to others, to the world.

She was also the one who brought me music. She loved music of all sorts, and her respect for artistic license cleared the way for my own artistic freedom.

So it is despite the darkness and the waiting, or in the heart of these, that the solar side developed and brought me to myself and to artistic creation.

*CFilippi*

# PORTRAIT
# OF MY MOTHER
MARTINE FRANCK ❖ PARIS, FRANCE

Here my mother is younger than I am today. A curious
sensation. From her, I learned a love of nature, and the
desire to reach formal beauty.

*Martine Franck*

# BALTIC, JULY 1911
GISÈLE FREUND
PARIS, FRANCE

This photograph was taken in Westerland on the Baltic in July 1911. I sit in front. I am two and a half years old. Around me, from left to right: my brother, Hans; our school teacher, Miss Schone; my father, Jules, in the center, wearing a summer suit; and his cousin, Felix Voss, on his left. My mother, Claire, is dressed all in white with a black bow, and sits next to her cousin, Frida Voss, and Frida's son on the left.

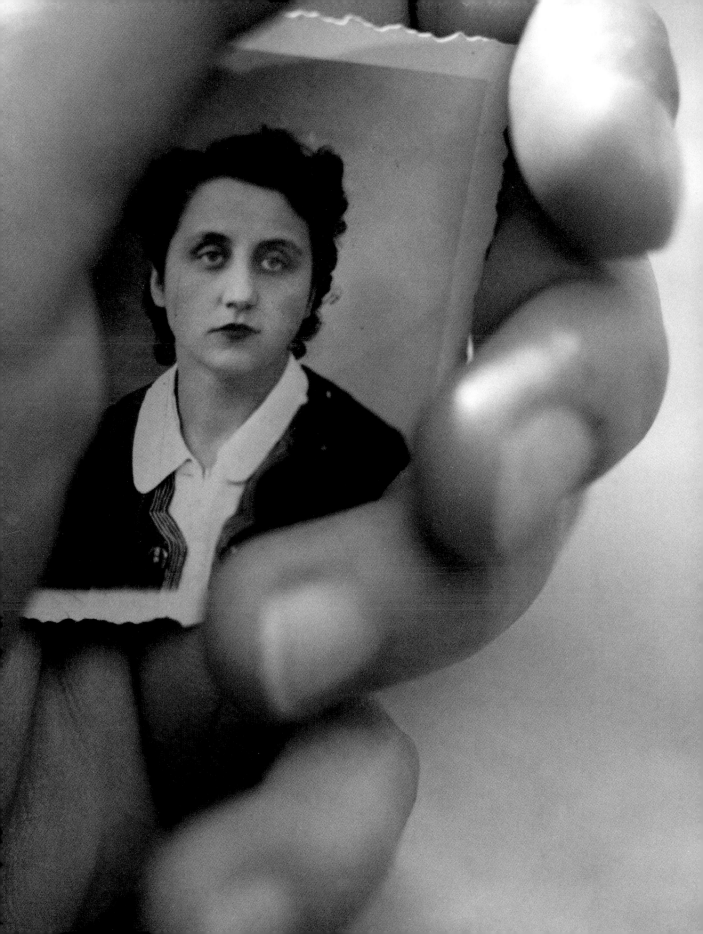

# MY HAND PROTECTS HER MEMORY

ANNE GARDE ❖ PARIS, FRANCE

This photograph I am holding in my left hand is a passport photo of my mother taken in the 1950s. My hand protects her memory.

She inspires in me a feeling that I still can't completely explain: a mixture of restraint and a desire to possess.

A rushing torrent I would like someday to control.

Something I do not know. Perhaps the mystery of disappearance between "never again" and a "déjà vu," a disquieting sense of existence which for me is a sort of signal—the very purpose of photography.

*Anne Garde.*

# WATER
# AND LIFE

FLOR GARDUÑO
STABIO, SWITZERLAND

My mother is a mystery to me. I associate her with life and water. We ourselves are for ourselves. I am a mother too: maternity is a mystery. Maybe one day my daughter Azul will say about her mother: Flor is like the water that gave me life.

*Flor Garduño*

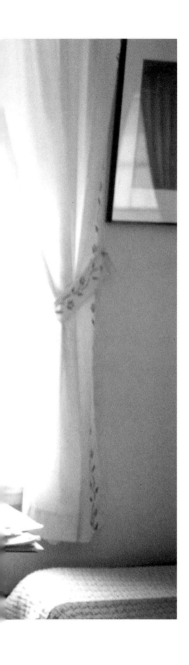

# LIL

NAN GOLDIN ❖ NEW YORK, NEW YORK

I used to be afraid of becoming my mother. That fear motivated me to travel as far away as I could in a certain direction. I thought drugs were the assurance that I was different. Now becoming her doesn't seem like such a bad fate. Because she no longer threatens my identity, my persona, either public or private, I am able to adore her in the way she deserves. She's very special—sensitive, fragile, proud, intelligent, sexy. Also a bit eccentric. She seems twenty years younger than her age in her energy and desire for experience.

My mother is a true survivor.

# THE INTIMACY
# OF THE LENS

Ekaterina Golitsyna ❖ Moscow, Russia

My mother is too humble to allow her presence to dominate a photograph. She is afraid of the intimacy of the lens. I could never catch all of her. And I cannot imagine her in any landscape other than that of the houses and canals in the dusty, spread-out city of the old St. Petersburg that she loves so much.

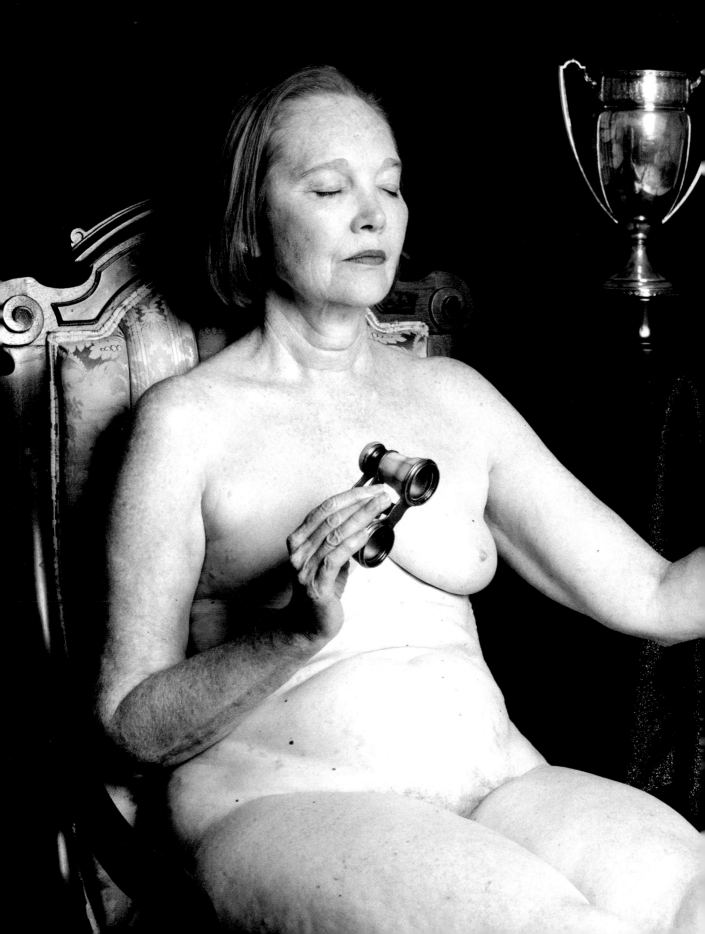

# MY MOTHER'S TOUCH

Deborah Hammond ❖ San Francisco, California

I remember lying in the darkness of my bedroom,
listening to the sounds of the house, and my mother,
moving quietly and deliberately, through all the rooms.
I could imagine her gently touching each object along
her path, so like a caress. The door to my bedroom
was ajar. My skin was ready. Soon it would be my turn
to feel the hand of my mother.

# ELENA

Tana Hoban ❖ Paris, France

This photograph of my mother in peasant dress is the one I most cherish. Her best friend is seated beside her. It was taken by a photographer in Ostroh, in the Ukraine, on November 10, 1909. She was only fourteen at the time. On the back of the photograph, the Russian inscription reads:

> *After many, many years going through bric-a-brac,*
> *one finds this pale picture, covered with a thick*
> *layer of dust; one may leave it without attention. . .*
> *But the opposite may happen, when one sees the*
> *picture of an old friend, one will take a cloth,*
> *clean it from the dust and sensitively look at it.*
>
> *One will remember the childhood friend who may*
> *not be around anymore, but it will be pleasant to*
> *remember the person who was close to you with life*
> *ideas. Look. Remember. For eternal remembrance*
> *to the revered friend Gochban.*
>
> Elena

Elena translates into Jennie, my mother's name, and the "revered friend" was, of course, my father. She must have given this photograph to him when she sailed for America in 1910, fearing she might never see him again but laying claim to his heart.

I like to remember my mother this way—spirited, warm and wise.

*Tana Hoban.*

# A LOVE
# FOR LIFE

Sara Holt ❖ Paris, France

Virginia Holt, my mother—
she's a great artist, she has
generosity, strength, she is
spontaneous and full of love
for life.

*Sara Holt*

# THE FACE OF DESIRE

IRINA IONESCO ❖ PARIS, FRANCE

As a little girl I was deprived of ever seeing my mother. I was entrusted into someone else's care. Because my mother was afraid I would be killed, she never acknowledged me as her own. She left for faraway countries where stares are shattered by oblivion. My eyes were totally burnt by the splendor of her obscure world.

Absent.

Someone else undertook to give me eyes that became my own.

I long for death and I am constantly dying from blindness.

Behind my closed eyes, a parallel world takes shape. A wandering world.

I am sitting on a Byzantine carpet which draws me relentlessly toward its rambling spirals. I am continually dazzled by the complexity of its patterns and its offer of a magical journey. I practice hypnosis. I learn how to give shape to her. I look for her. The Byzantine carpet is very obedient to forbidden stares. It leaves the face of desire on my retina—which is never satisfied and therefore endlessly repeated.  HER.

*Irina Ionesco*

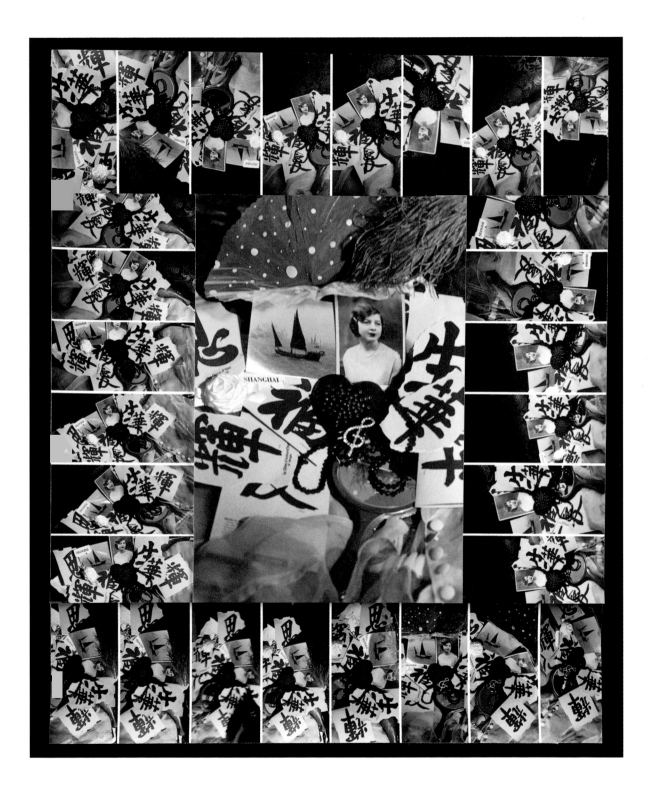

# PORTRAIT

FRANÇOISE JANICOT ❖ PARIS, FRANCE

My mother had an imperceptible quality. I was not able, even at a very high speed, to photograph her. So I drew her portrait, probably with the help of a passport photograph and from memory, as I used to do with dear friends.

This photograph of my drawing represents my mother in the 1950s.

*Françoise Janicot*

# MY MOTHER'S EMPTY CLOSET
MARION KALTER ❖ PARIS, FRANCE

**A**bove is my first photograph: I am seven years old. My mother handed me the camera to take the image. We were on a beach in Portugal. I remember that I was shaking while pressing the button. The photo is a little blurred.

My mother died nine years later. Little by little, I started taking photos in the house where I grew up. I never had a chance to photograph my mother, even though I had the impression I did it many times.

I spent a lot of time in her bedroom, looking through her clothes and trying them all on. When I finally had the courage to empty the closet, I could still picture my mother taking out her beautiful dresses, putting away the sweaters by color, and looking for the matching gloves. Then it was time for her appointment at the dressmaker.

Today, January 27, 1994, she would have been seventy-one years old. Within a year, I will be the same age as my mother was when she died.

*Marion Kalter*

73

# THE PAST REVISITED

Barbara Kasten
New York, New York

An oak tree stands alone where a home once existed. My grandmother, Barbara Budryte, was born in that home in Lithuania in 1876. At the turn of the century, she and her sister left their parents and a brother for a new life in the United States. They never returned. My mother, Julia, was born in Chicago in 1908. Nearly a century later, in 1993, my mother and I visited Lithuania for the first time and encountered an unknown branch of the family tree.

My mother immediately recognized her cousin because, she said, "She looks like my mother." I struggled to find the family resemblance, but my eyes saw only features that looked like the faces of my youth in Chicago.

On a bedroom wall in one of her cousin's homes, there was a photograph of her sisters and their families who survived two world wars and years of separation. As she held the photograph, the tears in her eyes made it clear that my mother was reliving a moment of her girlhood.

I've always been curious about the grandmother who never held me in her arms.

That trip to Lithuania with my mother linked me to the generations that had come before me. As my mother and I shared the past and created a new memory for the future, our own mother-daughter bond grew in mutual understanding, love and respect.

*Barbara Kasten*

JASCHI KLEIN ❖ HAMBURG, GERMANY

"The lady fakes interest, but she
really wants to read."

*Jaschi Klein*

# MY MOTHER
# AND HER SISTERS, 1925.

JO LEGGETT ❖ SAN FRANCISCO, CALIFORNIA

My mother, Cecil *(right)*, was the oldest of the three. She is the only one remaining. Leonore *(left)* succumbed to rheumatic fever the year this photograph was made. Her death became my grandmother's curse: a mother never recovers from the death of her child.

When I was very small, I remember nesting under the dining room table and imagining I was Leonore, dying and rising up to heaven like Little Eva.

The war was raging in Europe and Hitler was killing all the Jews. My parents were supposed to rescue and adopt two little sisters but they disappeared and were never heard from again.

For years, Selma *(front)*, who was always called 'Baby' by her parents, struggled hysterically to accept the terrible reality that her husband Jacques was missing in action. He never returned. My grandmother had a nervous breakdown. There was a constant flow of war news and soldiers; so many soldiers coming

and going in and out of my life. Well, it was hard to have much importance in the scheme of things; there were so many other compelling events and so many needy people.

This photograph of my mother and her sisters has always haunted me. Such a beautiful and peaceful moment, the calm before the storm.

At fifty-three, Selma chose to take her life rather than try to put it together again after a divorce—younger woman, you know. She was still very, very beautiful. I have gotten close to both of her daughters.

My mother is eighty-one and at peace with herself and her life. It is only when she hears that a mother has lost a child, then it all becomes unbearable for her.

And me? I too am a mother, divorced—a younger woman, you know. My offspring, although young, are grown. Contentedly, I have been able to let them go, to fly, to soar.

*Jo Leggett*

ANNIE LEIBOVITZ
NEW YORK, NEW YORK

This photo was taken on the
occasion of my parents' fiftieth
wedding anniversary.

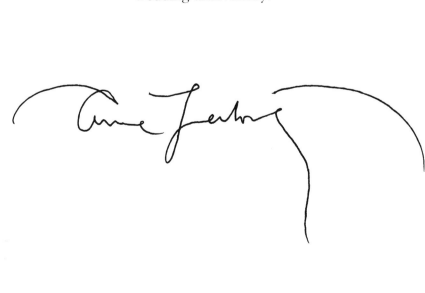

KODAK TX 5063   KODAK TX 5063

30A   31   31A MY MOTHER in MARIN 32A 33

Elizabeth Lennard

# MY MOTHER
# AND PHOTOGRAPHY

### Elizabeth Lennard ❖ Paris, France

My first assignment in photography class at the San Francisco Art Institute was to photograph someone close to me—my mother, for example. We were to use a plastic Chinese camera called a Diana which cost three dollars and took only black and white film. This was in 1970. I was living with my mother in the Presidio in San Francisco, and I remember the portrait I took with that camera. Of course, I don't know where the negatives or the prints are today.

Now, once again, I have been asked for a portrait of my mother.

To my knowledge, the first portraits of me were taken by my mother. In my family, it was my mother who took the pictures. My father always told us to notice architecture.

The way I picture myself as a child is based on the pictures my mother took of me. They strike me as being excellent family snaps.

My mother brought up three children, taking photographs and occasionally painting watercolors and some oils of them. All three of her children became photographers.

Here is a photograph of my mother taken on the beach in Northern California, where she lives now and where we go for walks when I come to visit her from Paris, where I live. The photograph is black and white and painted in oils. It makes me wonder whether Mom didn't influence my way of working. In the picture, she looks cheerful, happy to see her daughter.

I don't take many pictures of my mother. Parents always complain that their children take them for granted. They are probably right.

I don't take many souvenir pictures. Photography has been so much a part of my life for so many years that I don't have to use it as proof that I was in a certain place. I believe this is what inspires most amateur photographers who, when they find themselves at a beautiful spot, must photograph their next of kin in front of it. I don't find it necessary to use photography as a way of remembering; it has always been a way of creating.

*Elizabeth L*

# IN MY HEART

ARIANE LOPEZ-HUICI
NEW YORK, NEW YORK

### EVELYNE LOPEZ-HUICI

Beautiful . . . Adorable . . . Superb
Sweet . . . Radiant smile
Tender glance . . . Patient . . . Cheerful
Poetic . . . Desirable . . . Unconscious
Passage . . . Hymn of love . . . DEAD.
You were thirty years old. I was ten.
You are still in my heart.

*Ariane Lopez-Huici*

# THIS IMAGE OF MY MOTHER

Lea Lublin ❖ Paris, France

From all the portraits of my mother, I've reframed this image. The surrounding edges are torn, I am at her side at the age of one year, in order to fix a still, happy moment of fusion between two bodies joined in the memories of birth.

From this image of my mother before her body was torn, suffering, sick, unhappy, almost psychotic, I've kept the words she asked me to follow:

"Do what you want, follow the road that is yours, so that you arrive at your own happiness . . ."

It was her desire that I have a different future, one that achieves my own desires.

From her infinite love, from the words she urged me to follow, now that she is no longer here, I can tell her that in driving away from her, I was able to accomplish my own wish—her wish.

*Lea Lublin, 1995*

# THE DREAMER'S BIRTHDAY

MARI MAHR ❖ LONDON, ENGLAND

This work is part of a larger series entitled *Between Ourselves,* which is about my grandmother, my mother and my daughter.

"The Dreamer's Birthday" was created as a present for my mother. She was a lifelong humanitarian. The photos were made two years after her death and in the wake of the events in Eastern Europe.

Throughout her life, she firmly believed that communism could work. In an ideal world with no corruption, no nepotism, no greed or favoritism, her dream of true equality for all might have been achieved.

*Mari Mahr*

# MOTHER'S CUPBOARD

DOLORÈS MARAT ❖ PARIS, FRANCE

We were three daughters and a son. During the summer, our holidays had a special schedule. On Mondays, we did hand-washing. On Tuesdays, we ironed and sewed. Once those tasks were done and our arms were loaded with linen, my mother led us into her bedroom. Religiously, she opened her cupboard and we saw perfect piles of sheets, towels, cloths, white nightgowns, nylon underwear and bras with stiff cups. She took the linen from us and ordered us to go away. She remained there by herself.

In the following days, we knit our winter jumpers while listening to songs and plays on the radio. Our finished jumpers were ugly, but my mother forced us to wear them.

Saturdays were devoted to housekeeping.

Weeks went by this way. On the occasional Sunday, Aunt Jeanette came with her husband and daughter from Paris and brought us cream cakes for dessert. After coffee, we would visit Aunt Geneviève who lived next door.

We traveled in a van; my father and my uncle in the front, women and children in the back on a kitchen bench. We laughed from our departure to our arrival, hoping for sharp turns that would squash us together. We made fun of our aunt who was afraid to get her high-heel shoes dirty.

On Sundays, if no one came to visit, we went to the garage and made ourselves comfortable inside the boss' black Citroën. My parents and my brother sat in the front, my sisters and myself, constrained by our dresses, were in the back. For hours, we sat in the car on red leather seats. My mother daydreamed aloud of owning the Citroën. My father, his hands on the wheel, didn't dare.

On stormy days, we chased one another with pans full of water all the way into the kitchen. Once we hit the cupboard and it collapsed, mixing gherkins with cherries in brandy, mustard with jam, flour with pastas and the spirits received as gifts that my mother kept for special occasions all over the floor. This game came to an abrupt end.

Still, there were bottles to pitch into the pond during the long afternoons.

Today, I visit my mother who still dresses with care. She lives in a sand quarry. After a few hours, when we have said everything to each other, she will take me into her bedroom and open her cupboard.

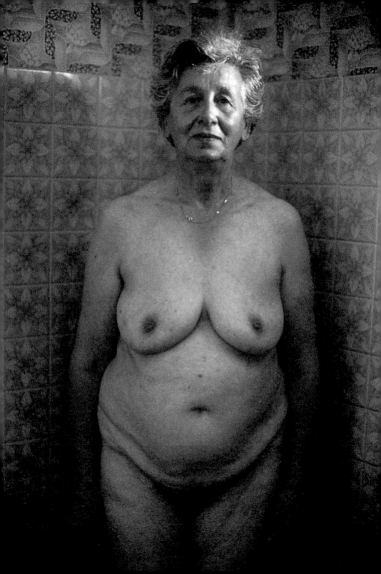

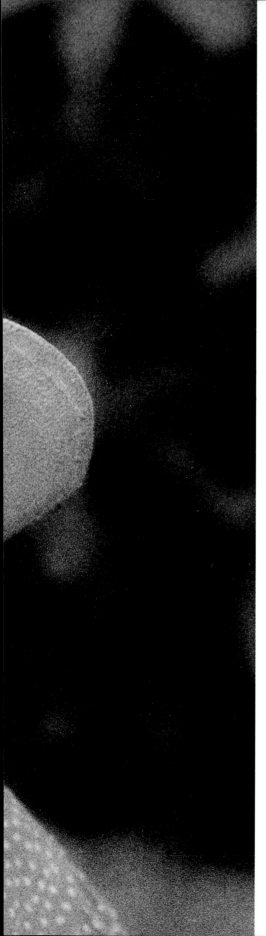

# IN THE SHADOW OF MY FATHER

HELEN MARCUS ❖ NEW YORK, NEW YORK

I took this picture of my mother in August of last summer. She and my father were sitting in the back yard of their house in Florida and I asked her to pose.

Mother is just ninety-three. She has raised four children and has lived in the shadow of my father all their married life. It is inconceivable to her to think of living without him.

She still tells me what to do. It amazes me that I continue to react exactly as I did as a child. It is very difficult for us to treat each other as equals. However, our relationship is changing. We are closer and warmer now.

Mother played the violin and the piano. I remember lying in bed upstairs as a child and always leaving my door slightly ajar so that I could hear her play.

When I sold my parents' house on Long Island last year, there was a piano that she insisted I take. After much urging, I took it and I even started taking piano lessons. I had not played since I was fourteen years old. My memories of having to practice were not particularly happy. I studied popular music then because Mother was studying it too.

Today I'm learning to play classical music. For the first time, mother and I play together. She plays the violin, I play the piano. We both tend to be hesitant when we play, but there is a warmth between us that wasn't there before. We now have a special bond that belongs only to us.

What a lovely memory. It will stay with me always.

*Helen Marcus*

# HER EYES NEVER LEFT ME

Corinne Mariaud ❖ Paris, France

Eyes watching me, for as long as I can remember.

Her eyes never left me.

A definitive and indestructible love

So weighty you can never fail it.

So strong it gives you the power of those who have always been loved

But the vulnerability of those who will always need to be loved.

# THIS PICTURE
# OF HER

Mary Ellen Mark ❖ New York, New York

My mother died many years ago. I never
knew her as a young woman because
when I was born she was already in her
forties. I always loved this picture of her. It
is a side of my mother that I never knew.

# JANUARY 1994.
# RECOLLECTIONS

SHEILA METZNER ❖ NEW YORK, NEW YORK

My mother Helen taught me to do things well and to love all kinds of work. When she finished cooking or sewing or knitting, she would kiss the tips of each of her fingers on both hands, saying as she did it, "Golden hands."

My mother believed she was the incarnation of an Egyptian queen. We had a statue of Nefertiti on the bookcase. The idea still lives deep in me.

My mother's album: Snapshots of her in a raccoon coat and a brown suede hat with feathers; in satin in her wedding picture; in a copy of a dress from a Joan Crawford film; in a bikini under a waterfall with handsome guys, laughing, a lot of makeup on her gorgeous face; wearing her hair in bangs, a chinoise face; wearing a red suit with a mandarin collar and beautiful round buttons. Even though the snapshots were glossy black and white, I remember the suit was red and the bathing costume was chartreuse.

At night, in the doorway to my bedroom, my mother would give me a "ticket to dreamland." She would kiss me and say, "Sweet dreams. Don't forget to say your prayers." I would carefully put my ticket under my pillow, say my prayers and lay down straight and flat, my arms at my sides. I would close my eyes and the next thing I knew I would be soaring, flying into the dark starry skies.

When my mother died, the dream ended. I came down from the stars to the earth. I was born.

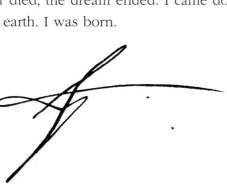

# TITTI

INGE MORATH ❖ ROXBURY, CONNECTICUT

My mother's name was Mathilde, but she was Titti to everyone, including my brother and me. What we admired most about her was that she could do so many things: Titti could do math, she knew flowers and trees by their Latin names and also how to plant, propagate and care for them. She was an excellent runner, swimmer and climber, and loved to work out on the parallel bars. She skied, piloted a glider and won fencing competitions.

THE RED KITE. DARMSSTADT, 1936.
My brother's school had its annual sports competition. Attending mothers wore sensible shoes, skirts and blouses. Titti appeared in a long white organdy dress, carrying a big red kite under her arm, which she intended to fly from an adjacent meadow after the event. Teenage boys don't care for flamboyance in relatives, but having been successful in the competition, my brother came along and allowed her to go first with her kite.

There she was, running in that long, fluttering white dress, hand holding the string raised high, head thrown back, looking at the kite flying in the wind above her. My brother says it did not fly very high, but I remember it did—way, way up.

Titti loved my professor father, Edgar. She worked with him in his chemistry lab with electron microscopes, coloring her slides of cell structures, creating little works of art. She corrected Edgar's papers, wrote some of her own. She was great at bandaging wounds. She had really wanted to be a surgeon but had to settle for pharmacology instead.

She could figure-skate and waltz to the left. She helped my father's doctoral students with their dissertations. She let admirers adore her from a safe distance. She allowed ballet dancers, for whom my father had a weakness, to lodge free in our attic rooms and thus, incidentally, advanced my gymnastic abilities through complimentary lessons.

PUNISHMENT. BERLIN, 1938.
We lived in a big house. The meals were handed through a small window-like opening from the kitchen into the dining room. French doors led from the dining room into the adjoining study. My brother and I were engaged in a big fight, knocking over a fragile Biedermeier table and then, in hot pursuit, crashing into the French doors. Titti, who was busy in the kitchen, heard the noise and called out.

We tried to escape, knowing that the

*In 1925, we lived in Munich and often went to bathe in a nearby lake. I did not know how to swim yet but adored the water and used an unguarded moment to walk straight into the lake. When Titti turned around, the tip of my head was about to disappear.*

*After the humiliation of the abrupt rescue, an accompanying friend asked to take a picture. I felt the request was beneath my dignity, but then, children were not supposed to contradict adults. Titti found the solution: I had to pose with her, but the way I presented myself to the camera was left entirely up to me.*

way from the kitchen to the dining room led through a winding corridor. But Titti simply jumped head-first through the serving hatch, landed in a roll on the floor, came to her feet and knocked our heads together with lightning speed. We accepted further punishment—a number of cuffs to our ears—in silent admiration.

*Inge Morath*

# SAVANNAH NANCE
## SEPTEMBER 15, 1917-JULY 12, 1995
MARILYN NANCE ❖ BROOKLYN, NEW YORK

My mother Savannah Nance, inspired in me a loving and a fighting spirit.

I was always sure that she had a much more interesting life than what she let on.

I recently showed her this picture that I had made of her and remarked that she looked like Harriet Tubman.

She asked me, "Did you know that Harriet Tubman and I are sisters? We were born in different times, but we're still sisters."

I looked at her for more information. She smiled and went back to manicuring her nails. I said to myself, "That's deep. I'm going to have to videotape her and get her story."

When she passed on, I grieved for that lost opportunity to sit down and talk.

Going through her stuff, I realized that my mother was a tracker. She tracked dates and events and assigned significance. She pretty much kept a file on all her folks, dead and alive.

It hit me. I do the same thing in my work; my sister does the same thing. We had always been carrying out her work.

We are just like her.

So, I publicly declare that I will *not* grieve over any historical or ancestral knowledge lost in the terror of Black life.

The way to knowing our ancestors is through knowing ourselves. We are so much like them.

Marilyn Nance

# WHAT I KNOW ABOUT HER

Janine Nièpce ❖ Paris, France

After a tramway accident, my mother was often bedridden with severe migraines. She died when I was four years old.

Three images captured by my eyes as if by a camera, remain fixed in my memory:

My mother is sitting next to me, on the staircase, near the playroom. A wardrobe falls, almost killing me. She is upset and tries to show her love to me. I am not so sure of it. I don't see her often enough. But in that moment, I know she is mine. She is tall, beautiful, looking elegant, even though she is wearing her dressing gown printed with bundles of violets and shoes with large white bows. I can touch her and smell her. I felt so pleased that the wardrobe fell! I'd have to make it happen again.

The second image is not so clear because I was half asleep. She came to kiss me. She was wearing the white sequined satin dress she always wore. The bedroom was bathed in candlelight. It was all so beautiful, I wanted to stay there forever.

The third image is of her burial. From behind the window, my elder sisters and I watched the guests, all dressed in black, standing in a circle in the garden. Once they noticed us, some of them started to cry. I will never forget the screech of the wheels of the hearse on the gravel.

At school everybody looked at me with pity. They would say, "That's the little girl who has no mother." I was different from the others.

Thanks to my father, my aunt and my sisters, I had a happy childhood. We never spoke of my mother. I never asked any questions.

Every year on All Saints' Day, we spent two days at my maternal grandmother's house. She was in perpetual mourning and never left her house except to visit her dead on All Saints' Day. Then she would lie on the tombs and cry. My godfather, who always held my hand, told me I was indecent because the socks I was wearing showed my ten-year-old ankles.

When we came home, we watched the little scenes from my mother's magic lantern. It helped to overcome my sadness.

I would also eat an enormous piece of St. Honoré cake and I always got ill. Then we would return to Paris.

During these stays, I learned my mother was a fervent Catholic. She'd made my father promise we'd be sent to a religious boarding school.

I admired my mother's paintings of bouquets of flowers and butterflies. There was a portrait of her done when she was twenty years old. I often looked at it to try to figure out who she was. I wanted to photograph the portrait of my mother along with one of me at the same age.

Janine Niépce

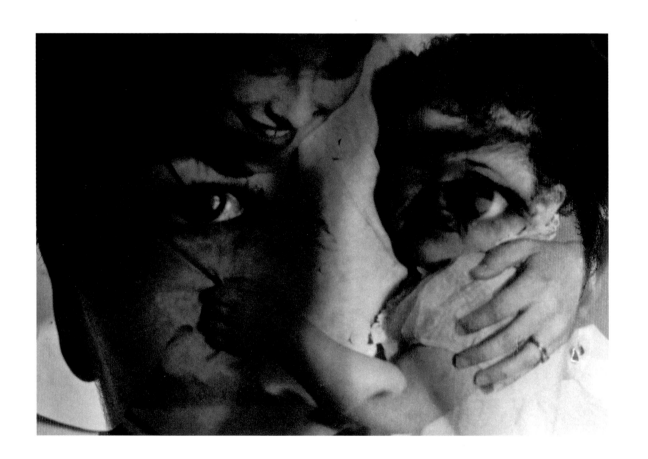

# CLUTCHING

PHOTOGRAPH BY LORIE NOVAK
BROOKLYN, NEW YORK

❖

TEXT BY SUSAN J. MILLER
CAMBRIDGE, MASSACHUSETTS

She is your momma, not mine. She's your memory, not mine. It's her cotton blouse you clutch. It's your little shoulder beneath the crisp, light sleeve, and your round upper arm that she presses with her wedding-ringed hand. It's her ring, her marriage, her husband.

It's my face you clutch, my skin you pull. It's my eyes yours look out of.

My daughter is eleven. She is silently growing her own story inside her, as you grew yours and I grew mine. What it will say I cannot guess. Someday she will tell it. Beneath my fingers her story grows, as minute by minute the stuff of it takes place.

These are your eyes. They are mine. Soon, she will see herself in them.

*Susan J. Miller*

# INSPIRATION

ELIZABETH OPALENIK ❖ OAKLAND, CALIFORNIA

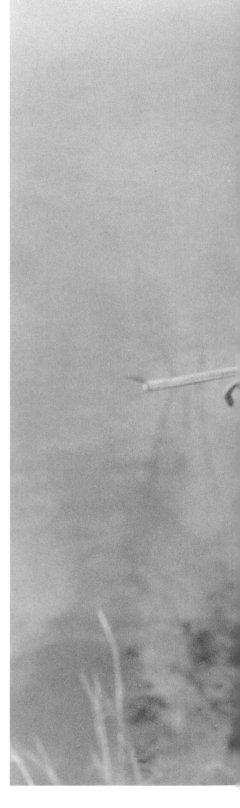

How sad I felt for everyone when I discovered that not all mothers in the world were like mine!

My mother had a kind word for all who passed through her farmhouse door. She was completely non-judgmental. If she didn't have a solution, she always had a hug and an encouraging word. For me, she was there to celebrate the triumphs, help to understand the failures and find inspiration in both.

She once told me, "I knew you were different from the time you were two." She has celebrated that viewpoint ever since.

The epitome of all good things that *mothering* universally implies, she was adopted by all who knew her.

On the day this portrait was made, a friend hired a stretch limousine to take his (and my) favorite mom to the airport. En route, there was a major traffic jam but the trucks allowed the limo to pass through. Excited to share her first limousine experience, she telephoned to report her journey.

"Those truckers must've thought somebody really special was in that limousine," she exclaimed.

"But Mom," I replied, "somebody really special *was* in the limousine."

To this day, there is no way to measure the amount of love and respect that I feel for this incredible human being. The most positive influence in my life, my mother remains a source of constant inspiration.

*Elizabeth Opalenik*

SUSANNA PIERATZKI
MUNICH, GERMANY

My mother is a woman of tremendous inner strength and love and I am grateful for being her daughter.

# DON'T BE AFRAID, BABY

Sylvia Plachy
Woodhaven, New York

The story goes that when my mother and father were young and hiking in the Carpathian Mountains, they heard the grunts of a bear. Before they started running, my father patted my mother on the cheek and said: "Don't be afraid, baby!"

On his deathbed he promised to wait for her.

Thirteen years later, bewildered by her own illness, she wanted to know, "What would your father say about this?"

"He'd say, 'Don't be afraid, baby!'" I answered.

It was October 1993, and my mother was very ill. By then I had forgotten my father's custom of bringing home a bouquet of autumn leaves. Some maple branches lay on a ledge outside my mother's building, already dry, pink and gold. When I brought the leaves inside to her, we both knew they were from my father.

My mother in 1980 after my father's funeral.

# STAR MODEL

Catherine Rotulo ❖ Paris, France

My beloved mother. Tender, loving. What can I say? She understood everything. She took me by the hand and led me to school, to piano lessons, to dance class, and to the museum. I admire her and we are still so close. It was always so difficult to leave home. I keep going back to be the little girl again.

My mother and I share our feelings, reassure each other, exchange ideas. We built a perfect unity. Through pain and grief, we have developed an exceptional, ever-renewing relationship.

Becoming an adult was a natural journey. I gained maturity, flew away and raced around the world but I came back to fetch my mother. I took her to America. We traveled in Mexico. We discovered Egypt and India together.

I am proud of her. She can be so demanding, but she can also be sensitive and generous, discrete and delicate.

I loved photographing her and getting to know her through my pictures. She is my star model with that magnificent face. I photographed her reflection in a mirror one morning by surprise. It was May 1990 on the island of Sorgue in the Lubéron.

# HELLO MOTHER!

Ernestine Ruben
Princeton, New Jersey

It's too late now . . .
         But
I always wanted
to ask you . . .
         Who *are* you?

                  Ernie
                  xxx

# IN MY MOTHER'S GARDEN
Jacqueline Salmon ❖ Lozanne, France

The most compelling portrait of my mother, without a doubt, was a photograph of her as a young woman with tilted head and a timid, yet seductive smile. She was the unknown woman with whom my father fell in love; the mysterious woman who was suddenly to become my mother.

I still have a light blue satin dress that belonged to her. This dress, girlish in color, slightly provocative with its low neckline, suits me. I wore it once. It shaped me, defined my hips, floated freely against my ankles.

Today there is this project. How should I portray my mother? And as a photographer, why have I never done it before? Many of my images are of my mother, but I somehow feel that those images of her face with a tense smile are not her portrait. Something is missing, something doesn't look right.

In my mother's garden, the nostalgia of childhood, the conscious or unconscious representation of paradise, her social position and her love of plants are all mingled together. Photographing my mother in her garden is my attempt to portray her in a natural landscape that is true to my emotions, my sincerity and the special bond between the two of us.

*Jacqueline Salmon*

# WHAT WAS SHE LIKE?

MELISSA SHOOK ❖ CHELSEA, MASSACHUSETTS

It took me years to realize that I remembered little of my childhood and virtually nothing of my mother, Sophia Antonia Shook. She died when I was twelve. I was never told she was ill; little was said about her death. My father soon sold the house and disposed of the furnishings. I was given her silver jewelry and the pink nightgown bought for the last week of her life. The following June, my father married the nurse who'd brought my mother home to die. Thereafter, he comforted himself with scotch until they were divorced.

I know what my mother looked like from snapshots in the family album. In my memory, she never held or kissed me, didn't make breakfast or pack my lunch for school, never read stories or tucked me in at night. I have no sense of her presence.

The experiences that led up to my own insecurity are hard to untangle. Inside, there is someone continually scolding me. I assume this is my mother's voice, but I don't know for certain.

What was she like? No one has ever told me. Perhaps she was reserved and distant, like my father, or maybe she was affectionate in subtle ways that were easy to overlook. Maybe the long illness caused her personality to shift and I got lost in the transformation. Maybe she was always demanding and severe.

I know something of her childhood from an aunt. She was one of five children born to German immigrants at the turn of the century. Sophie was dominated by her mother, an ambitious woman who invested in rooming houses before the Crash and then in a large hotel in Chicago. Her gentle, passive father, a sculptor of religious statuary, offered his children little protection against their abrasive mother. Family lore has it that each morning before school, he gave his daughters their hair ribbons, which he hid for them under the back stairs.

After my daughter Kristina was born, I began photographing her, our family, friends and the places we lived. My work developed from this impulse to preserve for my daughter what I didn't have for myself.

As a parent, I try to be a better mother to her than my father was to me. But now I understand that while his inability to protect and comfort me caused me deep insecurity, I profited from his independence of thought and intellectual drive.

However, I've never known what fears, beliefs, ideas and what strengths my mother passed along. I don't know who she was or what she gave me.

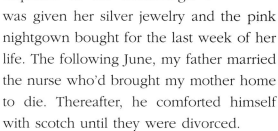

LAURIE SIMMONS
NEW YORK, NEW YORK

# GODDESS

SANDY SKOGLUND ❖ NEW YORK, NEW YORK

This is a picture of my mother in 1944, two years before I was born. I think she was extraordinarily beautiful, and I remember being terribly proud to be seen with her when I was a child.

She has now been buried more than twenty years, and it still wrenches my heart to conjure up her memory, so devastating and cruel was her death from cancer.

My parents had a very happy, loving marriage, and when my mother died, my father never quite got over it. He died fourteen years later of a heart attack.

My mother was smart, and exercised her intelligence with uncommon frankness. She had a powerful will and never complained while suffering from cancer. I found her dignity awesome.

In 1949 both my brother and I were struck with the polio virus. My brother did not suffer permanent paralysis but my left shoulder was deeply affected. The muscles were so reduced that the doctors were afraid I wouldn't be strong enough to hold up my arm. They wanted to pin the bones together permanently which would've left me with an immovable arm.

My mother would not allow them to perform the operation. Being a nurse, she insisted on trying a then-experimental treatment of exercising the muscles through physical therapy. Today, few people would ever notice that I had any kind of paralysis at all. There is still severe weakness in my upper arm, but it hardly shows in my daily life.

My mother's name was Dorothy.

To me she was a goddess.

*Sandy Skoglund*

MOTHER & DADDY. SARASOTA, FLORIDA 1976

# MOTHER ALWAYS SAID

Rosalind Solomon ❖ New York, New York

Mother always said,
"Keep your feet
on the ground and
your legs crossed."

*Rosalind Solomon*

# MOM, MY DAUGHTER AND MY CAMERA

LISSETTE SOLÓRZANO ❖ LA HABANA, CUBA

Mom is in front of my daughter . . . she's going to do it . . . going to lean over her, perhaps she will give her a kiss, or fix her shoe. Mom and my daughter have remained, looking at each other, in the eternal present of the photograph. I think I am only the vehicle used by my mom to have my daughter or maybe I am like the little fence that is between the two of them, negotiable, able to be overcome, but present. I am both; I come from one and go towards the other. I am my mother and my daughter at the same time.

In the photograph, though, they are looking at each other eternally, without my eyes. So that I won't be absent, I push the button on the camera . . . and there we are, the three of us: mom, my daughter, and my camera.

# OUR HEARTS

CHRISTINE SPENGLER
PARIS, FRANCE

When my brother, Eric, disappeared, my mother's heart and my heart became heavy.

Since then, to hide her pain, she dyed her hair black and put on a mask, like a geisha.

I left. I went to the countries at war. To forget.

Our paths never crossed again.

*Christine Spengler*

# NOW AND FOREVER

Laurence Sudre ❖ Paris, France

You left us quite recently, and it is difficult to talk about you, about us.

I took this picture on Dad's seventieth birthday. Your family came first, your husband, your five children and your ten grandchildren.

In February 1992, your mother, our grandmother, would've been one hundred years old. You gathered

us together, with your brother and sister. You read us a letter that you wrote to show us how present your mother was for you; just as you are still present for me, now and forever.

My Grandmother

*L Sudre*

# WHAT WERE HER DREAMS?

JOYCE TENNESON ❖ NEW YORK, NEW YORK

This is a photograph of my mother and her twin sister. I've always loved this image because it looks timeless. Their short hair and simple clothing allow us to concentrate on the intensity of their expressions, perhaps to look into their souls.

Because my mother died when I was twenty-one, I never really had the opportunity to have a relationship with her as an adult. I regret this deeply.

When my mother died, everyone said she was like a saint, probably because she was such a sweet and kind person. However, I'm sure she was more complex than that, and I wish I'd had the opportunity to investigate those areas now that my own perceptual abilities have evolved and sharpened over time.

Who was she really, and what were her dreams? These are questions I can never answer. This is the void that can never be filled.

*Joyce Tenneson*

# TO MY MOTHER, AUGUST 18, 1994

BERNADETTE TINTAUD ❖ PARIS, FRANCE

Our two faces in the mirror
while she was dressing my hair.

Life:
the slow trudging along in order that this block will divide itself. To
pass from girl to woman and be able to become a mother.

Life:
other crossroads to find its truth.
To prove then that close to it one is a long distance from oneself but
that an indestructible carnal bond perpetuates the connection.

And to feel the legacy:
love, tenderness to convey.

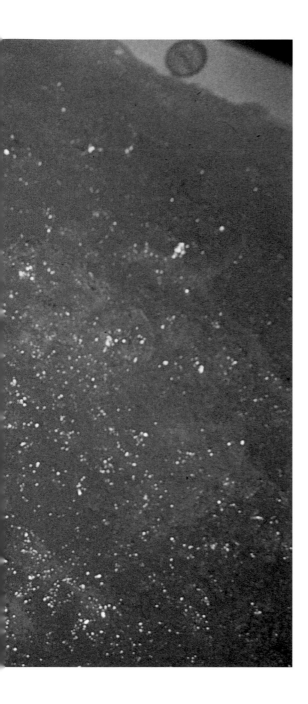

# SCARS

LINDA TROELLER
NEW YORK, NEW YORK

This morning, I recognize my mother's
face on my hand. Biting the corner of my
lip like she does.
Salt and pepper hair, flawless skin, nice red lips.
Bloodline similarities. The surgeon cut your face.
You've seen me pull myself in real small,
bending, crouching, shriveled.
The pain. The inner contents of a spray-can,
shaking in short, rapid, shivering movements.
Circles, surfaces, cones and lines.
My abdomen wrapped.
The blood.
What is the shape of your body?

*Linda Troeller*

# AND LIFE WENT BY

Yvette Troispoux ❖ Paris, France

I have vivid memories of my parents. They were beautiful people. I remember my admiration, watching my mother getting ready to go out with my father in the evening. I did not have a camera yet, but the image has remained with me. Tall, thin, with magnificent hair, wearing a lovely black satin dress with Luneville embroidery, black silk stockings and patent leather shoes.

As a child, when I was ill, I wanted her to stay with me. But her duties called her away. And life went by, with all its struggles, and the time came when she wanted me to stay with her all the time.

This is my favorite photograph. Favorite, because I succeeded in capturing one of her beautiful gazes.

*Yvette Troispoux*

# WHO I AM

Nathalie van Doxell ❖ Paris, France

I never knew a "mother." The woman who brought me into the world was not capable of looking after a little being so full of needs.

My mother was a very beautiful woman with a passionate temperament. She was always drawn to being somewhere else, attracted to someone else.

From the age of five or six, I became aware of her pathological lack of maturity. Instinctively, my reaction was to hate her.

Today, I feel a profound respect for her. I can understand the things that were impossible for her and I can appreciate the woman she was able to be.

Also, because of who she was and the needs she bequeathed to me, I became who I am, forever searching myself; therefore alive.

# SUNDAY AFTERNOON STORY

GUDRUN VON MALTZAN ❖ L'HAY-LES-ROSES, FRANCE

Looking through the window—from within or without.
A light yellow tablecloth is spread on an evenly mowed lawn.
Waiting for the guests, both big and small.
Adults resembling large, wet, hand-knitted pullovers and the children,

sticks of orange soaked in bitter chocolate.
It is sunny, everything is brightly colored and animated.
The customs and habits become stories and legends.
Ancestral porcelain plates are lined up, one after another.
Everyone has the right to nibble.
The plates still look good after all these years of delicacies.
Back to the tablecloth on the lawn.
Some string is attached to a corner.

If we follow it, we are led into the house, from room to room,
    story to story, up to the attic.
There, our investigation ends.
The other end of the string is attached to the tip of a smoked sausage.
Now people are pulling voraciously at the sausage, and at the same time,
    the yellow tablecloth on the grass flies into the air in front of the guests.
There is still time left to pick bouquets of small flowers as offerings of thanks.

*Gudrun von Maltzan*

# MISSING
# IN ACTION

Deidi von Schaewen ❖ Paris, France

This is a portrait of somebody who is not here anymore.

Life is a collage, especially hers. Her life revolved around the fact that my father was declared missing in action in Russia in 1943. She waited many years for him. In fact, she waited all her life. I can see her only through this fact. Such a tragedy, all the uncertainty, the endless waiting, the hope, the distress, the trying to live.

This was written in Paris on August 25, 1994, the day of the fiftieth anniversary of the liberation of Paris!

No to all wars!

*Deidi von Schaewen*

# AN AURA OF MYSTERY

ISABELLE WEINGARTEN ❖ PARIS, FRANCE

Florence Loeb, my mother, is a remarkable person who finds her children remarkable. I admire her appetite for life. I captured her beauty in my picture, almost by chance, a long time ago. On this image, an aura of mystery emanates from her. Although it doesn't come through in her demeanor, I see in it a kind of truth. Maybe because of this, a strong atmosphere of passion surrounds her.

*Isabelle Weingarten*

# FLIGHT

## Cuchi White ❖ Paris, France

Frankly, I find it extremely painful to write down my feelings about my mother. At least she cannot harm me anymore.

One essential problem of my generation is that our mothers wanted us to fit into a mold. It seems particularly ridiculous for anyone involved with the arts; anyone who doesn't care about appearances but only wants to achieve something in life, to die without a feeling of emptiness.

These mothers had no need to achieve anything that was worthwhile. At the age of fourteen, I was painfully aware of this yet unable to explain it. I had achieved nothing and I was unsure about my abilities. My mother did not comprehend it. She wanted me to conform to her ideas.

I had to escape to Europe to live my own life.

*Cuchi White*

# OUR COMMON CAUSE

NANCY WILSON-PAJIC
NOGENT-SUR-MARNE, FRANCE

It was about the time my father took this picture that I decided I wanted to be an artist like my mother when I grew up. Art was our common cause. I copied her drawings and we took lessons together.

Some years later, she had to choose between her social and family responsibilities on the one hand, and her ambitions as an artist and an autonomous individual on the other. Sharing her suffering made me aware at a very young age of the difficulties I would face as a woman artist.

*Nancy Wilson Pajic*

# BIOGRAPHIES

**Vivian Esders** was born in Paris and educated at the Business School H.E.C. In 1979 she opened the Vivian Esders Gallery, one of the first photogalleries in Paris.

A well-known dealer in contemporary photography, Esders has organized over 200 photo exhibitions through museums and institutions worldwide and has been responsible for the debut of many American photographers. She also works as curator for the 13th district of the city of Paris and various institutions on a regular basis and has been collaborating on Paris' Biennal "Month of the Photo" since 1980. Her publishing credits include a compilation work featuring 85 photographers entitled *In Search of Father* (Paris-Audiovisuel, 1993), participation in the Russian and Latin American sections of the *Mondial Dictionary of Photography* (1994) with Larousse Editions, and numerous introductions to photography catalogs.

Esders is currently a photography expert for the Paris Auction House in the Hôtel Drouot and is working on a book featuring contemporary photography from private collections.

---

**Paola Agosti** was born in 1947 and lives in Rome. She has been a professional freelance photographer since 1969 and has traveled throughout Europe, Africa, Latin America, and the United States.

Her photodocumentaries have been published by many foreign periodicals and her work has been shown in several solo and collective exhibitions, including "Volto d'autore" in Torino and "L'Italia fuori d' Italia" in Rome, projects which she personally edited. Some of her work is in the permanent collections of the Musée de l'Elysée in Switzerland and the Museo Nacional de Bellas Artes in Argentina.

Agosti is also the author of several photographic books, including *Mundo Perro* (Rome, 1993) and *Mi Pare un Secolo* (Torino, 1992).

**Sung Keum Ahn** was born in Korea in 1958 and graduated from the College of Fine Arts at Hong Ik University. Since 1979 she has been participating in numerous group and solo exhibitions and performances in Seoul, Berlin, Rome, Eindhoven, Tokyo, Milan, London, and Kwangu, Korea.

In 1985 she won the Grand Prize at the Tokyo Arts Festival, and her work can be found in the collections of the Museum of Hong Ik University and the National Museum of Contemporary Art, both in Seoul, and the Casa de Cultura in Bellreguard, Spain.

Ahn has been living in Paris since 1986.

**Barbara Alper,** a New York-based photo artist and freelance photojournalist, has been photographing for nearly twenty years. Her work is broad and diversified and includes her series entitled "The Gulf Channel," a commentary on the Gulf War and its media coverage made from an English-subtitled French network news broadcast and exhibited at the Victoria and Albert Museum in London in 1995.

Alper's work has been published and exhibited extensively in Japan, Europe, Scandinavia, and the United States and included in the collections of the Victoria and Albert Museum, the International Center of Photography, Maison Européenne de la Photographie, the Brooklyn Museum, and the New York Public Library, as well as private collections.

**Emily Andersen:**
"In my photographs, I am using the world to construct and project my vision, trying to capture the essence of feeling and place.

"I am concerned with issues of post-modernity, particularly in the unfixed identities contained within familial relationships.

"I have collaborated in making art works, and I live and work in London."

**Raymonde April** was born in 1953. She spent her childhood in Rivière-du-Loup, Quebec, Canada and studied visual arts at Laval University in Quebec City.

Throughout the twenty years of her career, April has shaped various photographic genres into her own personal expressions. Using images of herself and the people around her as well as cities and landscapes, she connects both the familiar and private.

Her work has been published and exhibited widely in Quebec and Canada, as well as France, Italy, and Spain.

She lives in Montreal where she teaches photography at Concordia University.

**Jane Evelyn Atwood** was born in New York in 1947 and has been living in France since 1971. Represented by Contact Press Images since 1988, she works primarily in documentary photography, following individuals or groups of people (usually those on the fringes of society) for long periods of time. She is the author of three books—two on French prostitutes in Paris and the other on the French Foreign Legion. She has won various international prizes and was the first recipient of the W. Eugene Smith Award in 1980 for her work on the blind. In 1987 she won a World Press Prize for the subject, "Jean-Louis—Living and Dying with AIDS."

In 1990 she was the recipient of the *Paris Match* Grand Prix du Photojournalisme and in 1991 was granted the Canon Photo Essay Award for her work on women's prisons in the U.S.S.R. In 1994 she was awarded a grant from the Hasselblad Foundation in Sweden and received the Ernst Haas Award from the Maine Photographic Workshops, U.S.A., to continue her work on women's prisons around the world. Her photos may be found in private collections and museums and have been exhibited internationally. Her first retrospective, "Documents," at La Villette, was part of the "Month of the Photo" in Paris in 1990-91.

**Aliza Auerbach** was born in 1940 in Israel where she studied at the Hebrew University and later taught high school. In 1972 she decided to become a professional photographer and worked in still life for major film productions around the world through the invitation of Gregory Peck in 1973 and William Friedkin in 1976. She has freelanced for all Israeli newspapers as well as for the *New York Times,* the *London Times,* and *Die Zeit.*

Her publishing credits include appearances of her work in *Family of Women* and *Family of Children*. She has also collaborated with Yehuda Amichai on his *Jerusalem Poems*. Her recent books include *Richonian* and *Aliya*, and she is currently working on two new books: *Motherhood Around the World* and *Working Women Around the World*.

**Dominique Auerbacher** was born in Strasbourg in 1955 and lives and works in Paris. Of her numerous showings, the latest is "May of the Photo" in Reims. Among her publications are *Les Quatre Saisons du Territoire* (1990) and *Fragments* (1993). She uses photographic images, video, and language codes to study modern aesthetics. She takes an inward approach with her video performances by adopting and exhibiting different personalities and placing them in various situations of everyday life.

**Carole Bellaiche,** born in 1964, began her career at the age of thirteen, photographing black-and-white portraits of young models. In 1985 she began a series of movie star portraits which were shown in Paris in 1994. Her photographic research deals with personal portraits, cities, ambiance, and the blending of people and places.

**Rossella Bellusci** was born in Calabre, Italy in 1947. She studied psychology after which she worked as a photographer at a Milan press agency. In 1978 she completed a documentary project on Native Americans on reservations.

Her work has involved extensive exploration of male nudes, still life, and auto-portraiture. In 1985 one of her photographs made the cover of the first issue of *Vogue Homme International Mode*. She completed her series "Lumieres frontales" in 1994.

**Agnès Bonnot,** the daughter of a cavalry officer, was born in the Drôme region of France in 1949. Due to the diversity of her studies, her early professional life was not deeply rooted. Bonnot was a model, comedian, stuntwoman, horseback- riding instructor, and a nude dancer at the Moulin Rouge. Her photos began appearing in the seventies and her first distinguished work reflected a horse theme. She won the Nièpce Prize in 1987. She is highly sought after for portrait and documentary work and among her publishing credits are the books *Horses* (1985), *Secret Faces, Discreet Looks* (1990), *Paris at School* (1993), and *Foot of Feather, Foot of Lead* (1994).

**Marlo Broekmans,** born in Holland, is self-taught in photography and has also studied psychology. She works mainly in black and white because she feels "it is so essential; it deals with light and dark, in the mystical and the psychological sense."

Self-portraiture is her main theme in which she attempts to "stage the self" and allow it to embody or incarnate a myth as seen in her catalogue "La Femme-Lumière" (1989). She has also completed documentary work on the *saddhus*, or holy men, of India and Nepal.

According to Broekmans: "I'm a dreamer who seeks realization through the camera."

**Vita Bujvid,** a Ukrainian born in 1962, decided to pursue a career as an artist despite objections from her family. She graduated from Dniepropetrovsk State University, where she worked on animation films. In 1990 she moved to St. Petersburg and began painting in oil but later changed to photography. In 1992 she won first prize for young talent in art photography in Russia. She has participated in group exhibitions held in Moscow, London, Berlin, St. Petersburg, and

the United States, as well as holding solo exhibitions at the Moscow State Museum and the De Moor in Amsterdam, among others.

**Chila Kumari Burman** is a visual and installation artist, photographer, filmmaker, writer, and performer. Born in Liverpool, she is currently based in London. Her work has been exhibited in the United Kingdom, Europe, Canada, Cuba, and the United States. A persistent theme in all her work is her determination to reclaim authorship of representations of Asian women by obliterating dominant and enduring stereotypes and images. A monograph on her work has recently been published by Kala Press and the Institute of New International Visual Artists (INIVA). Her mother died in 1995.

**Denise Colomb** was born in 1902. A gifted cellist, she moved to Saigon with her husband and children in 1935 when her passion for photography was born. In 1948 she joined the organized mission for the 100th anniversary of the abolition of slavery. Her portraits of Antonin Artaud (1947) marked the beginning of her series of artists' portraits that were the theme of her career until 1992, the same year she was named Knight of the Legion of Honor. Colomb has had numerous exhibitions, and today continues to be a prolific artist.

**Judy Dater** is a native Californian, has been the recipient of two National Endowment for the Arts Fellowships (1988, 1976), a Guggenheim Fellowship (1978), and the Dorothea Lange Award (1974). Her work is housed in the collections of the Metropolitan Museum of Art, the Museum of Modern Art, the International Center of Photography, all in New York City; the Boston Museum of Fine Arts; the University of California, Los Angeles; the Toppan Collection, Tokyo Metropolitan Museum of Photography; and the Bibliothèque Nationale, Paris, among others. Dater's solo exhibitions have been held at the San Francisco Museum of Modern Art; the Victor Hasselblad Aktiebolag Gallery, Sweden; the Contemporary Arts Center, New Orleans; and the Oakland Museum. She has also appeared in numerous group exhibitions.

Her publications include *Cycles; Body & Soul: Ten American Women; Judy Dater: Twenty Years; Imogen Cunningham: A Portrait;* and *Women and Other Visions: Photographs by Judy Dater and Jack Welpott.*

**Simone Douglas:**
"My work is primarily concerned with aberrations, the things that are absorbed but not instantaneously recognizable. I am interested in colliding realms of the memory and the imaginary in tilting the axis of meaning. My work contains things that are in our field of vision if we choose to seek them out.

"The images are the question; the answer lies in the flight of the eye."

**Sandra Eleta:**
"Photography to me has been like an intimate diary in which images and life have danced together into the same rhythm. My photos on Portobelo—an old historical seaport on the Caribbean coast of Panama where I have lived for many years—has been my most meaningful work. In making the portraits of this wonderful people—descendants of ex-slaves who came from Africa during the Spanish Conquest—I could experience the possibility of nearness, an insight into their souls. This feeling opened up a way for me to reach out and converse with life. Without this gift, I wouldn't be able to drink the juices of a full existence."

**Corinne Filippi,** of Italian and Gypsy descent, lives and works in Paris, where she studied philosophy and dance. After her involvement with various dance forms, Filippi became a photographer. She has had individual and group exhibitions in France and abroad. According to Jean-Jacque Levêque, "Dance has given her a taste for radical commitments, work with the body, sensual contact with matter. Through photography, she takes us into the very heart of matter, into its vibrations. It is the art of stealing the secrets of the world."

**Martine Franck** was born in Antwerp, Belgium and raised in the United States and England. She studied at the University of Madrid and at l'Ecole du Louvre in Paris. In 1964 she worked in the Time-Life laboratory in Paris and was also assistant to Eliot Elisofon and Gjon Mili. Franck began her freelance career in 1965. She has been a full member of Magnum since 1983.

**Anne Garde,** with her books and her international exhibitions, creates images of events that extend beyond realism—images that express a kind of hypnotic truth. From *Villégiatures* (Colona Editions, Paris, 1982) to *Hué, Vietnam* (Demi-Cercle Edit. Ministry of Culture, Paris, 1994) to *The China Club* (David Tang, Hong Kong, 1994), her landmarks are connected to a double transformation, through memory and through the photographic secret.

Her work traces varied themes, from industrial, as in *Images des Lieux en Lorraine (*Beaubourg Museum, 1988) and *Factories in Burgundy* (Government commission, 1994), to her study on European taste in India as seen in her *Salon Indien,* for which she received the Villa Médicis Grant.

**Flor Garduño** was born in Mexico in 1957 and studied visual arts at the School of Fine Arts at the National University in Mexico City and at the atelier of Kati Horna, assisting Maestro Manuel Alvarez Bravo in the printing of three important portfolios using the platinum process. Through 1980-86 she worked as a freelance photographer and in art-work reproduction, publishing her first book, *Magia del Juego Eterno* (1985). In 1987 she followed with *Bestiarium*. Garduño won Switzerland's Federal Grant for Applied Art in 1993 for her very successful project "Witnesses of Time," which toured in the United States, Mexico, and Europe. Her latest book is *Mesteños* (1995).

**Nan Goldin** was born in Washington, D.C. in 1953 and began studying photography at the age of sixteen.

In the late seventies her renowned evolving slide show "The Ballad of Sexual Dependency" was shown in galleries, film festivals, and museums throughout the United States and abroad.

Goldin has exhibited her photographs worldwide, including at the Museum of Modern Art, New York; the Whitney Museum of American Art; the Museum of Fine Arts in Boston; the Centre d'Art Contemporain in Geneva; and the Folkwang Museum in Essen, Germany. She has received grants and awards from the Tiffany Foundation, Cameral Austria, the National Endowment for the Arts, and the D.A.A.D. in Berlin. Her photographs and writing have been published in numerous international anthologies and magazines.

Her publishing credits include *Cookie Mueller* (1991), *The Other Side* (1992), *A Double Life* (1994), *Tokyo Love*, and *Desire by Numbers*. Goldin lives in New York.

**Ekaterina Golitsyna** was born in Moscow in 1964 and later graduated from the Moscow Book Publishing and Printing Institute with a degree in graphic art and book design. She began her freelance photography in 1990 and is a member of the Russian Union of Art Photographers.

Golitsyna has participated in many exhibitions in her native Russia and elsewhere.

**Deborah Hammond** has spent the majority of her years living and working in San Francisco. For more than a decade she has concentrated on portrait-based black-and-white photographs. She has exhibited her work across the United States, Europe, and the Middle East.

**Tana Hoban** has been a photographer and illustrator ever since she graduated from the Moore College of Art in Philadelphia. For years she was best known for her photographs of children, appearing in magazines and advertising. Since 1970 she has photographed and designed over forty-five children's books, some of which have been published outside the United States. Her most recent book, *Little Elephant*, features her own daughter's words.

Hoban has held many exhibitions in the United States and France, including a show at New York's Museum of Modern Art.

**Sara Holt,** sculptor and photographer, was born in Los Angeles, California in 1946. She received her B.F.A. at the University of Colorado in Boulder.

Holt has produced sculptures inspired by her light and color experiments in connection with her long-exposure photography of the night sky. She has worked with different materials and has been commissioned for many outdoor sculptures in France.

**Irina Ionesco** was born in Romania and currently lives in Paris. For many years, her photography centered only on a black-and-white format, favoring baroque and theatrical settings, with only women or her young daughter Eva as subject matter.

Ionesco has authored seventeen books and her work has been shown throughout the world. She is presently involved in her project, "Desire for the Orient," dividing her time among Paris, Cairo, Alexandria, and the Mauritanian Desert.

She has begun introducing color into her photography.

**Françoise Janicot,** painter, photographer, and performance artist, lives and works in Paris.

Since 1959 she has held individual exhibitions of her paintings worldwide, including shows in Paris, Madrid, Anvers, New York, and Vaduz. Her photographic works have been shown through various exhibits since 1973, and she has recently sold ten of her photographs to the Fonds National d'Art Contemporain in Paris. Her publishing credits include *Poésie en Action* (Loques/Nèpe Publishers).

**Marion Kalter** has always traveled extensively, even as a child, although exotic subjects never held an interest for her. She has always focused her work on what existed around her and within her.

Kalter loves the austerity of black and white. She is especially touched by family portraits and representations of the themes of "generation" and "roots."

Within recent years, Kalter has specialized in photographing the world of classical music.

**Barbara Kasten** has held exhibitions in the United States, France, Lithuania, Poland, Japan, Spain, and Turkey. She has photographed worldwide landmark architectural sites, including the Puye cliff dwellings in New Mexico and the ancient Roman ruins of Tarragona, Spain. She has received a Fulbright Hays Fellowship, a John Simon Guggenheim Fellowship, and a National Endowment for the Arts Grant to direct and produce *High Heels and Ground Glass,* a video documentary about five female photographers of the twentieth century. Kasten is also a recipient of an Apple Photo Grant, a program that fosters creativity in computer imaging. She lives and works in New York City.

**Jaschi Klein** has studied both photography and painting and has been exhibiting her work since 1976, having held shows throughout Europe as well as in Japan and the United States. She has also completed two experimental films and collaborated with Michael Engler on several documentaries filmed in the United States and Middle East. Since 1980, Klein has been teaching at various art academies and conducting free workshops throughout Europe.

**Jo Leggett:**
"I developed my first roll of black and white film in 1975 and carried the negatives in my bag, offering to show them to anyone willing to look. I was hooked. Throughout the seventies and eighties I studied, learned, and made images of my daughter as she was growing up. As that project became increasingly foreboding, I moved on to color and my study of sentience in livestock, a quality not usually attributed to animals.

"I am in the process of becoming the publisher of *Photo Metro* magazine and having the time of my life.

"My mother died on March 15, 1995 at the age of eighty-three."

**Annie Leibovitz** is a contributing photographer to *Vanity Fair, Vogue,* and *The New Yorker.*

**Elizabeth Lennard** is a photographer and filmmaker who lives and works in New York and Paris. She has shown at major galleries in the United States and Europe, including a one-person show at the Centre Georges Pompidou in Paris.
". . . Lennard works with the memory of a visual moment, examining the feeling which was concealed and which she then fastens to the interior of the picture by reinforcing it with color."—Nathalie Leleu

**Ariane Lopez-Huici** was born in Biarritz, France and currently lives in New York City. She has held many exhibitions including solo shows at the AC Project Room in New York, the Kunst Station Sant Peter in Cologne, and the Museum of Photography in Los Angeles. She has also participated in group shows throughout the United States and United Kingdom.
"Ariane Lopez-Huici photographs the *exultate jubilate* of the bodies, the pleasure, the erotism after the discovery in India of the Laksmana temple of Khajuraho. . ."—Michel Nuridsany

**Lea Lublin** was born in Argentina and currently lives and works in Paris. She has been teaching at l'U.F.R. d'Arts Plastiques et Sciences de l'Art of the University of Paris since 1977. She received a research scholarship in visual arts from the Guggenheim Foundation for 1984–85 as well as a FIACRE scholarship from the Délégation Arts Plastiques in 1992. Her numerous solo exhibitions include the recent "Memoire des lieux–Mémoire du corps" (1995). Her most recent participation in a collective show was "Féminin–Masculin" at the Centre Georges Pompidou in Paris.

**Mari Mahr** was born in Santiago, Chile and studied at the School of Journalism in Budapest. She worked as a photojournalist in Hungary before moving to London and receiving a degree in photographic arts at the Polytechnic Institute of Central London. In 1989 she was awarded the Fox Talbot Prize by the National Museum of Photography, Film & Television.
Her work is in the collections of many museums including the Bibliothèque Nationale in Paris, the National Gallery of Australia, the Contemporary Art Society, and the Arts Council of England, both in London.
Her solo and group exhibitions have been seen in galleries and museums throughout the world, including England, Holland, Germany, Greece, Scotland, the United States, Spain, and Italy. Mahr lives and works in London.

**Dolorès Marat** was born in Paris in 1944. Self-taught, she began concentrating on her personal work in 1983 after terminating a long collaboration with the women's magazine *Votre Beaute,* "to remark on what no one had noticed, the lady in red on a subway bench, the cowboy at the movies, the blinking of a nuclear warhead, or a department store neon." In 1994 she received the European Publishers Award for Photography, the jurists of which later published her work. In 1995, *Rives,* her volume of 104 photographs, was published.

**Helen Marcus,** a freelance photographer based in New York, specializes in corporate portraiture, annual reports, and food and travel around the world. Her work has appeared in the *New York Times, Time, Food & Wine, Travel & Leisure, Gourmet,* and *Publishers Weekly,* among other publications.
She has held solo exhibitions at the Asia Society, the New York Public Library, *Parents Magazine,* and the Overseas Press Club. Her work is in the collections of the International Museum of Photography and the International Center of Photography, both in New York and the Museum Ludwig in Germany.
She currently teaches at Parsons School of Design.

**Corinne Mariaud** was born in Paris in 1964 and studied at Les Arts Appliqués Duperré from 1982 to 1986. Between 1987 and 1991 she worked as an advertising art director. She is currently a photographer for the French press, doing portraits and illustrations.

**Mary Ellen Mark** has achieved worldwide visibility through her numerous photo-essays and portraits in such magazines as *Fortune, GQ, Harper's Bazaar, Life, Mirabella, Rolling Stone, New York Times Magazine, Vogue,* and the *London Sunday Times.*
Her images of the world's diverse cultures have become landmarks in the area of documentary photography; these include her portrayal of Mother Teresa and a photo-essay on runaway children in Seattle which became the basis of the Academy Award-nominated film *Streetwise.*
Mark has received many awards, most recently the John Simon Guggenheim Fellowship, the Matrix Award, and the Dr. Erick Salomon Award. She holds an honorary Doctor of Fine Arts degree from her alma mater, the University of Pennsylvania, as well as from the University of the Arts.
Mark's photographs have been exhibited worldwide and she has published nine books, including *Indian Circus* (Chronicle, 1993).

**Sheila Metzner** studied at Pratt Institute in the early sixties and started her career as the first woman art director at the Doyle Dane Bernbach ad agency in New York. For the past twenty-two years she has distinguished herself with her fine-art photographs, editorial and advertising assignments, exhibitions, and books.
Her work has also been featured in magazines such as American, French, British, and German *Vogue, HG, Travel &*

*Leisure, The Traveler, Interview, Vanity Fair, Harper's Bazaar,* and *Amerian Way*. She has worked on special assignment for films, directed television commercials and her own short film on the artist Man Ray.

She has been exhibited internationally and her fine-art photography is in the collections of the Metropolitan Museum of Art, the Museum of Modern Art, the International Center of Photography, the Museum of Fine Arts, Houston, the Chrysler Museum, and the Agfa and Polaroid Corporations.

**Susan J. Miller** lives in Cambridge, Massachusetts with her husband and two children. Her essay "Never Let Me Down" appeared in *Granta #47*. She is currently working on a memoir to be published by Henry Holt.

**Inge Morath,** born in Austria in 1923, has been a member of Magnum Photos since 1953. She works as a photographer for various magazines, including *Life, Paris Match,* and *Holiday.* She has also published a number of photographic books including *From Persia to Iran, Venice Observed, Portraits, Russian Journal,* and *Spain in the Fifties.* Her next book, on the Danube River, is due out in October 1995.

Morath has held individual exhibitions at many museums, including the Art Institute of Chicago and the Royal Photographic Society. She received an Outstanding Accomplishment Award from the state of Michigan in 1983 and a Certificate of Appreciation from the Smithsonian Institution in Washington, D.C. in 1985. She is an honorary member of the Austrian Museum of Photography and winner of the Great Austrian State Prize for Photography in 1992. She resides in Connecticut.

**Marilyn Nance** is a photographer/storyteller known for her work on African-American spiritual expressions. A resident of New York City, Nance studied graphic design and photography at Pratt Institute, photojournalism at Empire State College, and video, digital imaging, and the history of photography at the Maryland Institute, College of Art.

She received two New York Foundation for the Arts Fellowships (one in photography and another in non-fiction literature) and has been an artist-in-residence at Light Work and the Studio Museum in Harlem.

Her photographs have been published in *The Black Photographers Annual,* the *New York Times, Life,* and *The History of Women in Photography* and are in the collection of the National Museum of American Art at the Smithsonian Institution in Washington, D.C.

Nance is currently interested in multimedia production.

**Janine Nièpce,** was born in 1921 and in 1947 became one of France's first women photojournalists.

During the sixties her work took her to India, Brazil, New York, and Canada. She has exhibited with Robert Doisneau and Willy Ronis and has also appeared in Peter Pollack's book, *The Picture History of Photography,* which had an accompanying show at the Smithsonian Institution.

In 1992 Nièpce held an exposition entitled "France 1947–1992" during the "Month of the Photo," and a solo exhibition at the Smithsonian Instiution in 1994. Her publishing credits include *France* (Janine Nièpce/Marguerite Duras, 1992) and *The Woman's Years: 45 Years of Images.* Her work has also been shown at the French Consulate in New York City.

**Lorie Novak** has been a recipient of both National Endowment for the Arts and New York Foundation for the Arts Fellowships. Her photographs and slide installations have been shown extensively, including in exhibitions at the Smithsonian Institution, the Museum of Contemporary Art in Chicago, the Museum of Modern Art in New York, the Art Institute of Chicago, the Houston Center for Photography, and Breda Fotografica in the Netherlands. Novak lives in Brooklyn and teaches photography at New York University's Tisch School of the Arts.

**Elizabeth Opalenik** is a fine-art, editorial, and commercial photographer whose work with extended print, infrared film, and the Mordançage process is exhibited and collected internationally. She has been teaching figure workshops and alternative processes in the United States, France, and Italy for over a decade, with portfolios and articles recently published in American and Italian *Zoom, Editrice Progresso, Photo District News, Photo Design,* and *Collectors Photography.*

Born on a farm in western Pennsylvania, she now resides in northern California.

**Susanna Pieratzki:**
". . . the basis of my work deals with philosophical and mystical aspects of society, which are expressed through a series of images that aim to enter into dialogue with the viewer. The main objective of my prints is to convey a clear and understandable message, which is achieved through the complex yet minimalistic imagery of my photographs."

**Sylvia Plachy** was born in Budapest and came to the United States with her parents after the Hungarian Revolution. She lives in New York with her husband, Elliot Brody. They have one son, actor Adrien Brody.

Plachy is a graduate of Pratt Institute and a Guggenheim Fellow. She has been a staff photographer at the *Village Voice* since 1976. Her monthly column "Signs and Relics"—two pages of words and pictures—appears in *Metropolis* magazine. Her book of photographs, *Unguided Tour* (Aperture) won the ICP Infinity Award in 1991 and was traveled by the Minneapolis Institute of the Arts.

Her photographs are in many collections, including George Eastman House, the Metropolitan Museum, and the Museum of Modern Art. Plachy has exhibited in solo and group showings worldwide. *Red Light,* a collaboration with Jim Ridgeway, is a book of photos and text about the sex industry and will be published in the fall of 1996 by Powerhouse.

**Catherine Rotulo** was born in Versailles, France in 1948. In her early youth, she studied music and dance and later studied law in Paris, after which she embarked on her photographic career.

In 1971 she held her first exhibition of the Maurice Béjart Dancers in Paris and afterwards became the personal photographer of French pop star François Hardy for four years. She has traveled extensively and produced work for many news and art magazines, including *Paris Match.*

Rotulo is now photographing portraits of French women writers and artists. She spends half of her time on the Ile de Ré, the "new St. Tropez of the Atlantic."

**Ernestine W. Ruben** has created works which blur the distinction between images and objects by utilizing a unique process which combines handmade paper with photographic images.

Her works have been widely published and exhibited in both Europe and the United States, and she frequently teaches intense workshops.

**Kathy Ryan** has been a connoisseur of photography for seventeen years and is the photo editor for the *New York Times*

*Magazine.* She has twice been awarded the University of Missouri National Press Photographers Association "Pictures of the Year" competition award for picture editing and has edited several photography books including *Feeling the Spirit: Searching the World for the People of Africa,* with photographs by Chester Higgins, Jr.

Ryan lectures regularly and spoke earlier this year at the Interfoto Conference in Moscow. She also enjoys teaching and has participated in the Eddie Adams Workshop and the Rich Clarkson Workshop.

**Jacqueline Salmon** was born in 1943 and studied history, visual arts, and architecture in Paris. Since 1981 the main theme of her photographic work has been the relationship between art, philosophy, and architecture. In 1993 she received the "Villa Médicis hors les murs" Grant.

**Melissa Shook** has centered much of her work on family life, beginning in 1965 when her daughter was born. Shook has also completed lengthy documentary projects, including portraits and interviews of homeless women—a project which evolved from her working or volunteering in shelters since 1982. She has received an NEA Visual Artist Fellowships and a MassProductions Grant. Her work is in the collections of the Museum of Modern Art, New York; Fotografiska Museet, Stockholm; and the Bibliothèque Nationale, Paris.

Shook is currently an associate professor in the art department at the University of Massachusetts, Boston.

**Laurie Simmons** is an artist/photographer who lives and works in New York City. Her work has been exhibited internationally and is included in the collections of many museums, including the Museum of Modern Art, New York; the Whitney Museum of American Art, New York; the Corcoran Gallery of Art, Washington, D.C.; the Museum of Contemporary Art, Los Angeles; the Stedelijk Museum, Amsterdam; and the Hara Museum, Tokyo. She is the mother of two daughters, Lena and Grace Dunham.

**Sandy Skoglund:**
"My work involves the physical manifestation of emotional reality. The invisible becomes visible, the normal, abnormal, and the familiar, unfamiliar. Ordinary life is an endless source of fascination to me in its ritualistic objects and behavior.

"In the process of working, I find great irony in exercising total control over the visual and dramatic elements. I restructure events by creating them from scratch, and force chance to blow things my way."

**Rosalind Solomon** is a widely published explorer, photographer, and printmaker who also creates installations and unique books. She began photographing at the age of thirty-eight and has studied with Lisette Model. Her works are exhibited and collected by museums throughout the world and have won her awards from the John Simon Guggenheim Foundation, the National Endowment for the Arts, the American Institute of Indian Studies, and Art Matters, Inc. Her projects in the United States, Latin America, India, and Africa include "Children of the 20th Century," "Survival and Loss," "Portraits," and "Landscapes." "Rosalind Solomon, Ritual," her solo exhibition in 1986 at the Museum of Modern Art, was curated by Peter Galassi. Solomon resides in New York City.

**Lissette Solórzano** was born in Santiago, Cuba in 1969 and studied both design and photography. She has participated in various international workshops and the Havana Biennial. Her work has been exhibited in New York, Sao Paolo, Caracas,

Curaçao, Milan, and Cuidad Metera, Italy. One of her photoessays was selected for the Casa de las Américas Prize in 1994. Her work has also appeared in numerous international publications.

**Christine Spengler** was born in France but raised in Spain and began her photography in 1970 with the support of her brother Eric. In 1973 she became one of the few woman war photojournalists working in Vietnam.

After hearing of her brother's suicide, she spent the next fifteen years photographing solely in black and white. Her "Mourning of the World" documented tragedy and suffering throughout Northern Ireland, Cambodia, Lebanon, Iran, Nicaragua, and El Salvador.

After working for SYGMA, Spengler published her first book, *A Woman in the War* (Ramsay, Paris, 1991). After years of contemplating her personal losses, she rediscovered color photography and worked for *Vogue,* Christian Lacroix, and Yves St. Laurent.

In 1992 she held a large retrospective entitled "The Opera of the World" which toured Paris, New York, London, Madrid, and Tokyo.

**Laurence Sudre** was born in 1950 in St. Etienne, France, and in 1969 studied with Claudine and J. P. Sudre.

Sudre's early work comprised wall and graffiti photography and numerous documentary projects. From there she quickly moved into portraiture, concentrating on actors, directors, comedians, and artists including Dennis Hopper, Wim Wenders, Pierre Amoyal, and Patrice Chereau. In 1989 she set up a photographic studio in the Palais des Festivals in Cannes.

**Joyce Tenneson** has participated in over one hundred exhibitions worldwide and her work is included in many museums and private collections. She is also a much-sought-after portrait, fashion, and beauty photographer with clients in Europe, Japan, and the United States. Her photographs have appeared in many major magazines, including *Premier, Esquire,* the *New York Times Magazine,* and French and Italian *Vogue.* She is the author of four books, of which the most recent, *Transformations,* includes an introduction by *New York Times* photographic critic Vicki Goldberg. In 1989 she won the International Center for Photography's Infinity Award for Best Applied Photography and in 1990, was named "Photographer of the Year" by the international organization, Woman in Photography.

**Bernadette Tintaud** has had her work shown throughout Europe since 1984. She feels her photographs are the result of a double origin: "The cliché of the original stems from reality; a raw matter that is then shaped to extricate a new form. The resulting 'look' is vigilantly maintained." Tintaud lives in Paris.

**Linda Troeller** is a New York City-based art photographer and photojournalist who won the Ferguson Award from the Friends of Photography in San Francisco for her worldwide touring project *TB-AIDS Diary* (1989). In 1992 she was awarded Picture of the Year for "Jacuzzi, Calistoga Hot Springs, California" from *Healing Waters* (which includes the portrait of her mother). This work features the growing trend of pilgrimages to ancient hot springs, healing sites, and spas.

Published in *Vogue, Life,* the *New York Times,* Troeller currently lectures and teaches workshops in Rochester, New York.

**Yvette Troispoux** was born in Coulommiers, France in 1914. Her very first photograph won her a Kodak Award in 1933, and in 1936 she left to work in Paris. Her passion for photography is still strong today. Called the "photographer of photography," Troispoux takes for her themes people and events as well as landscapes and architecture.

**Nathalie van Doxell** was born in 1960 in Paris where she studied art history at l'Ecole du Louvre in Paris. Her photographic images are intended to be symbolic rather than narrative, and by focusing her work on the geometric plane, she explores the potential of the inherent enlargement and reduction qualities of photography. Her themes concentrate around personal, social, and political relationships as expressed through her photographic representations of "surface" versus "deep."

**Gudrun von Maltzan** was born in Germany in 1941 and studied in Berlin and at the Academy of Fine Arts in Munich.

"I present a world of paradoxes. Paradoxes which initiate an art of metamorphosis and metaphor, immediately apprehended. My works refer to a lucid world. If they command such a direct approach it is due to the specific technique I developed through my decades of work. This technique rests less on use of today's socially dominating media, and more on an older, more traditional form of image recording dominant during its day: painting."

**Deidi von Schaewen,** was born in Berlin, studied painting at the Hochschule fur Bildende Kunste in Berlin, and worked as a designer and photographer in Barcelona from 1970–1974. During that time she also worked in New York as a camerawoman and subsequently as a film director. Since 1974 von Schaewen has been working in Paris as a photographer for international magazines covering architecture and design.

Her exhibitions have been held in Paris, New York, Berlin, Amsterdam, and Barcelona. Her film credits include *Man Ray,* which she co-produced with the Centre Georges Pompidou in Paris in 1984, and *Roland Roure,* which won a prize at the 1984 International Festival of Art in Montreal. Her two books are *Walls* (1977) and *Echaffaudages, Structures Ephemeres* (Paris, 1992).

**Isabelle Weingarten** is currently a portraitist and still-life photographer for film. It was through her early professional work as a model that she became interested in taking her own photographs, enlisting her friends and family as models. This was followed by acting on stage and in films by Bresson, Eustache, Manuel de Oliveira, and Wenders. She worked on portraits for *Les Cahiers du Cinéma.*

**Cuchi White** was born in Cleveland in 1930. After graduating from Bennington and exhibiting in "This Is the Photo League," she moved to Europe and married Italian painter Paolo Boni. Her publishing credits include *L'Oeil Ebloui, Reveuse Riviera, Villages Perchés,* and *Sentier des Douaniers en Bretagne.* She has also exhibited at the Venise Biennale and at the "Neopolis-Metropolis" during the annual G7 world economic conference. She has been living in Paris since 1954.

**Nancy Wilson-Pajic,** born in Indiana in 1941, played an important role in the avant-garde of the seventies with her pioneering installations and text works. In 1978 she took up residence in Paris, where she created a unique imaging system based on pigment emulsions with which she produces large-scale, permanent images on canvas. Recognized as a precursor of the French "Photographie plasticienne" ('artists photography') movement, her work has been presented in three major museum retrospectives, one of which was in the Musée national d'Art moderne, Centre Georges Pompidou, Paris, in 1991.

# CREDITS

**Page 1:** © 1996 Photography Anne Garde, Paris. **2:** © 1987/1995 Ernestine W. Ruben. **3:** © 1996 Catherine Rotulo. **4:** (top to bottom) © 1996 Paul Bergen; ©1996 Aliza Auerbach; "Self Portrait," © 1996 Denise Colomb; © 1996 Mary Ellen Mark; © 1996 Inge Morath; © 1988 Elizabeth Opalenik. **5:** (top to bottom) © 1996 Linda Troeller; © 1996 Corinne Filippi; © 1995 Marilyn Nance/Reprinted by permission of Marie Brown Associates; "Julia," © 1994 Barbara Kasten; © 1990 Judy Dater; "Virginia Holt," © 1994 Sara Holt. **6–7:** Photos by Scott Thode. **8:** Photo by Lionel Fourneaux Photographe. **10:** Photo by Roberto Pera. **11:** © 1995 Paola Agosti. **12–13:** (left) "An Image of Buddha" © 1994 Sung Keum Ahn; (right) © 1996 Sung Keum Ahn. **14:** © 1995 Claude Alexandre. **15:** © 1996 Pierre Jacquin. **16–17:** (both) © 1996 Barbara Alper. **18:** © 1996 Emily Andersen. **19:** Photo by Sunil Gupta. **20– 21:** (both) © 1996 Raymonde April. **22–23:** (left) © 1995 Gueorgui Pinkhassov; (right) © 1996 Jane Evelyn Atwood. **24:** © 1996 Eden Auerbach-Ofrat. **25:** © 1996 Aliza Auerbach. **26:** *Ma Crotte en Chocolat* video, Paris © 1993 Dominique Auerbacher. **27:** "Self Portrait," © 1990 Dominique Auerbacher. **28:** © 1996 Carole Bellaiche. **29:** Photo by J. M. Grangier. **30:** © 1996 Rossella Bellusci. **31:** © 1993 Rossella Bellusci. **32–33:** (left) © 1996 Agnès Bonnot; (right) Photo by Louis-Martin (Bonnot's five-year-old son). **34–35:** (left) "The Voyage," Self Portrait, © 1988 Marlo Broekmans; (right) "Portrait of My Mother," © 1988 Marlo Broekmans. **36–37:** (left) Photo by Edward Stranadko; (right) © 1996 Vita Buijvid. **38–39:** (left) © 1996 Chila Kumari Burman; (right) Photo by Christine Parry. **40:** "Self Portrait," © 1996 Denise Colomb. **41:** Photo by Denise Colomb © 1996 Ministère de la Culture, France. **42:** © 1990 Judy Dater. **43:** "Like Mother Like Daughter," © 1994 Judy Dater. **44–45:** (left) © 1994 Simone Douglas; (right) © 1995 Simone Douglas. **46:** © 1996 Sandra Eleta. **47:** Photo by Sylvia Grunhut. **48–49:** (both) © 1996 Corinne Filippi. **50:** © 1996 W. Ronis/Magnum Photos. **51:** © 1996 Martine Franck/Magnum Photos. **52–53:** © 1996 Gisèle Freund. **54:** © 1996 Photography Anne Garde, Paris. **55:** © 1996 Irina Ionesco. **56–57:** (left) © 1996 Adriano Heitmann Fotografo; (right) © 1994 Flor Garduño. **58–59:** (left) © 1993 Nan Goldin; (right) Photo by Christine Fenzl. **60–61:** (left) © 1996 Ekaterina Golitsyna; (right) © 1994 Ekaterina Golitsyna. **62–63:** (left) Untitled (Loving Cup), © 1993 Deborah Hammond; (right) © 1996 Deborah Hammond. **64:** © 1996 Tana Hoban. **65:** © 1995 Gail H. Alexander. **66–67:** (left) "Virginia Holt," © 1994 Sara Holt; (right) Photo by Jean-Max Albert. **68:** Photo by Christine Spengler. **69:** © 1996 Irina Ionesco. **70:** © 1994 Françoise Janicot. **71:** Photo by Nathalie de saint Phalle. **72–73:** (all) © 1996 Marion Kalter. **74–75:** (left) Photo by Corky Nault; (right) "Julia," © 1994 Barbara Kasten. **76–77:** (both) © 1996 Jaschi Klein. **78–79:** (left) © 1996 Jo Leggett. **80–81:** (left) © 1996 Paul Bergen; (right) © 1996 Annie Leibovitz. **82–83:** (left) © 1996 Elizabeth Lennard; (right) Photo by Erica Lennard. **84–85:** © 1996 Ariane Lopez-Huici. **86:** © 1996 Lea Lublin. **87:** Photo by Ernesto Monteavaro Fotografo. **88:** "The Dreamer's Birthday/3," © 1991 Mari Mahr. **89:** (both) © 1996 Mari Mahr. **90:** "Self Portrait," Paris © 1995 Dolorès Marat. **91:** © 1996 Dolorès Marat. **92–93:** (left) © 1993 Helen Marcus; (right) © 1996 Helen Marcus. **94–95:** (both) © 1996 Corinne Mariaud. **96:** © 1996 Mary Ellen Mark. **97:** Photo by Grant Delin. **98–99:** (both) © 1996 Sheila Metzner. **100:** © 1992 Peter Baum. **101:** © 1996 Inge Morath. **102–103:** (both) © 1995 Marilyn Nance/Reprinted by permission of Marie Brown Associates. **105:** (top) © 1993 Janine Niépce; (bottom) Photo by Robert Doisneau. **106:** © 1991/1994 Lorie Novak. **107:** Text from "Never Let Me Down," *Granta* #47/Reprinted by permission of Susan J. Miller. **108–109:** © 1996 E. R. Martinez; (right) © 1988 Elizabeth Opalenik. **110–111:** (left) © 1990 Susanna Pieratzki; (right) © 1996 Susanna Pieratzki. **112–113:** (both) © 1996 Sylvia Plachy. **114–115:** (both) © 1996 Catherine Rotulo. **116–117:** (left) Photo by Photographies Karl Kugel; (right) © 1987/1995 Ernestine W. Ruben. **118:** © 1993 Jacqueline Salmon. **119:** © 1996 Jacqueline Salmon. **120:** Photo by Ellen Haynes. **121:** © 1996 Melissa Shook. **122:** "Mother/Nursery," © 1996 Laurie Simmons/Metro Pictures. **123:** (both) © 1996 Laurie Simmons/Metro Pictures. **124–125:** (both) © 1996 Sandy Skoglund. **126–127:** (left) © 1976/1996 Rosalind Solomon; (right) © 1996 Rosalind Solomon. **128:** © 1996 Lissette Solórzano Lopez. **130:** © 1996 Christine Spengler. **131:** Photo: Ph. Warner/Ch. Spengler. **132–133:** (all) © 1996 Laurence Sudre. **135:** © 1996 Joyce Tenneson. **136–137:** (left) "Passage," © 1996 Bernadette Tintaud; (right) © 1996 Bernadette Tintaud. **138–139:** (left) © 1996 Linda Troeller; (right) Portrait by Silvana Martinelli. **140:** © 1991/1996 Yvette Troispoux. **141:** "Self Portrait," © 1996 Yvette Troispoux. **142:** © 1993 Nathalie van Doxell. **143:** Photo by Marco Delogu. **144:** © 1993 Gudrun von Maltzan. **145:** Photo by Gabriel Silgidjian. **146–147:** (both) © 1996 Deidi von Schaewen. **148–149:** (left) © 1995 Isabelle Weingarten; (right) © 1996 Isabelle Weingarten. **150–151:** (left) © 1996 Cuchi White; (right) Photo by Luigi Ghirri; **152–153:** (both) © 1996 Nancy Wilson-Pajic.